Samuel: The Untold Chronicles

A Complete Journey Through the Life of the Prophet Samuel

by Gary E. Risenhoover

Published by Kinetic Digital Publishers

www.kineticdigitalpublishers.com

For permissions, inquiries, or other correspondence, please visit our website.

ISBN eBook: 979-8-90235-111-5
ISBN Paperback: 979-8-90235-112-2
ISBN Hardcover: 979-8-90235-113-9
LCCN: 2026908895

TABLE OF CONTENTS

Whispers from the Tabernacle: The Birth of Samuel 3

In the Shadow of Eli: Childhood Among the Priests 15

The Night When Heaven Called: Samuel's Divine Awakening 33

A Judge Rises: Steering Israel Through Turmoil 43

Anointing the First King: Saul's Crown and Collapse 62

The Shepherd and the Ages: The Advent of David 78

Prophet and Kingmaker: Samuel's Solo Compass 91

Legacy Carved in Stone and Spirit 107

The Heart's Calling: Lessons from Samuel's Life 120

Bridging Judges to Monarchs: A Transformative Era 134

Concluding: A Thank You to You 151

Hey there, Amazing Reader!

Welcome to a journey unlike any other, where curiosity meets passion and ideas burst into life! This book was born out of countless late nights, fueled by endless cups of coffee and a relentless desire to dive deep into the topics that ignite minds and spark change. From the very first spark of inspiration, I knew this wasn't just another book—it was a mission.

Crafting these pages took dedication, research, and a wild ride through unexpected discoveries. Whether it was poring over obscure studies, interviewing brilliant minds, or wrestling with complex concepts, the process was nothing short of exhilarating. Each chapter is a carefully crafted piece of a bigger puzzle, designed not just to inform but to electrify your thoughts.

But let me be clear: this book isn't here to bore you with dry facts or endless jargon. Nope! It's packed with stories, insights, and moments of "aha!" guaranteed to keep you hooked. My goal? To make every page pop with energy and meaning, pulling you in deeper with every turn.

I took great care to ensure every idea here is backed by solid research, but told with a spark that makes it unforgettable. You'll find surprises lurking in each chapter, challenging what you think you know and inviting you to see the world a bit differently.

This book is a labor of love, crafted with the reader in mind. I want you to feel like you're sitting down with a trusted friend who's eager to share secrets, laugh, and explore. It's about connection, inspiration, and the thrill of discovery.

As you move forward, I encourage you to keep an open mind and let your curiosity roam wild. There's no rush—take your time, savor each idea, and let them marinate. Trust me, the payoff at the end is worth every second spent.

Whether you flip through the pages in one sitting or nibble slowly over weeks, know that this book is your companion. It's designed to challenge, amuse, and ultimately empower you.

Thank you for embarking on this adventure with me. I promise it's going to be a ride packed with surprises, insights, and moments that stick with you long after the last page is turned. So, buckle up and let's dive into a world where knowledge meets excitement in the most electrifying way possible!

With boundless enthusiasm and a spark of friendship,

Gary E. Risenhoover

Whispers from the Tabernacle: The Birth of Samuel

The Silent Prayers of Hannah

The hills of Ramah stretched out beneath a sky brushed with the soft hues of dawn, the ancient earth bathed in the gentle, amber light of morning. A sparse wind stirred the dry grasses, carrying with it the faint scent of wild thyme and the distant bleating of sheep beginning their daily wanderings. The landscape, rugged and weathered from decades of sun and scarce rain, held a quiet solemnity—an eternal backdrop to the daily rhythms of Israelite life. Amid this timeless scene, a lone figure knelt by the threshold of the tabernacle, a worn stone building that bore silent witness to countless prayers and whispered supplications over the years. This was Hannah, a woman whose heart was as heavy as the desert noon, whose silent prayers echoed the deep, yearning ache of a soul longing for a child. Hannah's anguish was not a fleeting emotion but a persistent shadow that clung to her being. The loneliness she carried was profound, as palpable as the dry earth beneath her knees. Years of barrenness had left her isolated, burdened not only by her lack of offspring but by the unspoken judgment of a community that prized motherhood as a measure of a woman's favor with God. In ancient Israel, the blessing of children was intertwined with divine approval, and those without it were often viewed with quiet suspicion or sorrow. To be barren was to live on the margins of hope, to bear an unacknowledged grief that no human consolation could assuage. Yet Hannah's prayers were not cries of bitterness or despair. They were whispered in the deep stillness of the night and the early hours of the morning, words formed in the silent sanctuary of her heart. Her lips moved no louder than a breeze, yet her soul spoke with a fervor that reached beyond the physical confines of the tabernacle, touching the very heart of the Divine. Sitting on a low stone bench in the shadow of the ark, she poured out her spirit in solitude, her eyes closed against the temptation to weep openly before Eli, the high priest, and the other pilgrims who had come to worship. Each prayer was a delicate thread woven from hope and desperation, humility and fierce longing. Hannah knew the customs, the sacrifices, the rituals. She had come to the tabernacle year after year, bearing her silent burden, bringing offerings that were as much an act of faith as an expression of her own yearning. But in her deepest moments, her petitions were stripped raw and simple, a pure plea to the God who sees what no human eye can perceive. It was in this sacred silence—between the measured beat of the priests' prayers and the sacred songs of the Levites—that Hannah bared her soul. The barrenness she endured was more than a physical reality; it was an existential trial that wore heavily on her spirit. In a society where lineage was the thread that connected each generation, where inheritance and identity flowed through sons, the absence of a child was to be cut off from the future itself. Friends and family, though kind in their own way, often spoke in hushed tones or avoided the topic altogether, as though the whisper of her pain would break the fragile walls of communal harmony. Hannah's husband, Elkanah, was a man of quiet strength and steady love, yet even his goodwill could not completely shield her from the persistent ache of childlessness. The socio-cultural pressures were relentless. At the annual pilgrimage festivals, when the assembly gathered to celebrate the great feasts before the Lord, Hannah found herself surrounded by women who carried babes at their breasts and toddlers toddling at their feet. The joyful laughter and shared tasks of motherhood, so natural to those blessed with children, widened the gulf of her loneliness. Each festival was a poignant reminder of what she lacked, a test of her faith to remain steadfast amid the chorus of blessings around her. Yet it was precisely this context that forged the steel of her devotion. Hannah's prayers were not demands cast into the void, but humble offerings of pleas and promises. She understood profoundly the covenant relationship between Israel and God, the binding oath to live in obedience and trust. Her silence was a language of reverence, her heart a temple of sacred petitioning. The ancient songs of the Psalms sung by the Levites echoed through the air: "The Lord is near to the brokenhearted," they intoned, giving voice to what Hannah dared not admit aloud—that her heart was fragile but not defeated. Her promise to the Lord was a vow born of desperation but rooted in faith. In the deepest recesses of her spirit, she pledged that if God granted her the gift of a son, she would consecrate that child back to the Lord's service all the days of his life. It was a radical act of surrender, a contract of hope made with no guarantee but full obedience. This vow was not born of bargaining but of trust—in the God who hears silence, who discerns the unvoiced prayers of a broken heart. The ambient stillness of the tabernacle grounds at dawn was pierced only by the rustle of elders moving through the courtyards and the low murmur of the first prayers of the day. Yet Hannah remained unmoved, anchored in a moment suspended between earth and heaven. The arid desert air, dry and sharp against her skin, seemed to hold its breath with her, as if the very elements awaited the unfolding of a divine mystery. Her eyes lifted briefly to the heavens, those endless stretches of blue that invited the human spirit to dream, to hope, to trust beyond all logic. In this sacred solitude, Hannah's innermost conflict was laid bare. Her mind wrestled with the pain of her condition—the social shame, the quiet sorrow, the sense of exclusion—while her heart clung fiercely to the promise of God's mercy. The repetitive nature of her prayers, the rhythm of her vows, became a lifeline in the desert wilderness of her soul. Each silent conversation with the Almighty fortified her against despair, weaving hope into the fabric of her daily life, strengthening her resolve to remain faithful amid the emptiness. Her husband, Elkanah, loved her deeply, yet even his words of comfort could not reach the depth of her struggle. He tried to reassure her each time their family gathered for a feast or a festival, reminding her of her beloved place in his heart. But Hannah's yearning was a private pain, a sacred fire that he could not quench. The separation between husband and wife, wrought not by lack of affection but by the cruel hand of fate, was a crucible in which faith was continually refined. Within the tabernacle's worn stones, something unseen was beginning to stir—an unfolding promise that would ripple through generations. Hannah's silent prayers were not merely private lamentations; they formed part of a larger divine narrative. They connected her to the lineage of the patriarchs, to the covenant of Abraham, to the enduring hope of Israel. The God she prayed to was not distant nor indifferent, but was intimately present in the depths of her longing, attentive to the words unspoken and the tears unshed. The sensory details of the setting—the sharp scent of burning incense mingled with sun-dried earth, the clear light touching the ancient symbols, the whispering palms that edged the water vessels—all carried a palpable sense of expectancy. The world seemed to hold its breath with Hannah, sensing the threshold upon which she stood. This expectancy was neither naïve nor facile; it was a mature hope born of struggle, tempered by years of quiet endurance. In this liminal space, between the visible and invisible, the sacred and the ordinary, Hannah's story embodies the universal human drama of hope against despair, faith amidst suffering, and the mysterious ways in which divine grace unfolds in the human experience. Her silent prayers, though unheard by most, resounded in the divine court, altering the course of history. As dawn gave way to morning light and the first calls to worship echoed through the hills of Ramah, Hannah rose with a heart both heavy and light—heavy with the burden of her longing, yet lightened by the courage of her faith. She stepped from the tabernacle's shadow into the surrounding world, where the ordinary tasks of life awaited, carrying within her a secret hope that one day would burst forth in the form of a child who would change the destiny of a nation. In the silence of those early morning prayers, amid the ancient stones and the whispering winds, the seeds of the prophet Samuel were sown—not only in the womb of a woman but in the very heart of Israel's destiny. And as the desert air warmed under the touch of the rising sun, the world waited with bated breath—witness to the silent prayers of a woman named Hannah, prayers that would echo through history as a testament to faith, hope, and divine mystery.

Eli's Encounter and the Promise Made

The air inside the tabernacle was heavy with the scent of burning frankincense and cedarwood, its ancient timbers whispering tales of devotion and sacrifice. Shadows crept along the worn flagstones as flickering oil lamps cast wavering pools of light against the rough-hewn walls. Every sound echoed softly beneath the vaulted ceiling, the solemn hush of a space consecrated far beyond mere human reckoning. It was within this dimly illuminated sanctuary, among the veiled places reserved for God's presence, that a woman named Hannah sought refuge with a heart burdened by longing and despair. Hannah's footsteps were careful and measured, as if she feared disturbing the holy stillness with her human frailty. Her hands, knotted tightly in prayer, trembled beneath a simple linen shawl, worn from years of hardship and heartache. She had come alone, leaving behind the noise and judgment of the crowded courtyard outside, seeking solace at the very altar where countless sacrifices had been made in the name of Israel's God. It was night, a time when the world grew still, and the veil between heaven and earth seemed thinnest, inviting whispered prayers and secret pleas. As she approached the sanctuary's inner recesses, her eyes fell upon a solitary figure seated near the priestly chambers —

Eli, the high priest of Israel. His aged face was creased with years of ministry and sorrow, carved like ancient stone into the worn folds of his robe. The flickering oil lamp beside him cast shadows that danced across his beard, lending his presence a mysterious and somber weight. The lines around his eyes told stories of battles fought not on fields, but within the heart: struggles between faith and frustration, hope and weariness. Hannah's heart beat faster, a pulse of anticipation mingling uneasily with humility. As a motherless woman burdened with barren sorrow, she had no place of her own sanctuary; the temple's holiness was both a beacon and a trial. Yet here she was, driven by an unbearable ache, her soul laid bare before the One who hears the silent cries of the spirit. "High priest

Eli," she began, her voice barely above a whisper but clear and trembling with earnestness, "I come to you not as a woman of prominence or wisdom, but burdened and broken. Grant me your ear, for my heart is grieved beyond measure. "Eli, whose years had taught him to discern many voices — from the boastful to the penitent — regarded her with measured eyes. His gaze was both faltering and searching, unsure in its first moments of the stranger's plea. In the quiet of the night, the weight of his priestly duties pressed upon him, and yet something within her demeanor stirred an unfamiliar compassion. "Speak, child," Eli said gently, his voice a rough whisper softened by age. "What troubles do you carry? Is your sorrow known to the Almighty? For He hears all prayers, especially those whispered by the brokenhearted. "Hannah took a breath, steadying herself against the tide of emotion rushing within. "My heart is my torment," she replied, the fervor of her words weaving into the fragile stillness like a sacred chant. "For years, I have prayed for a child — a son to call my own. Every festival, every offering, I have lifted my voice to the heavens, but still, the womb remains silent. Tonight, I have come with a vow in my heart, a promise I make before the Lord: if He will grant me a son, I shall dedicate him to His service all the days of his life — a Nazirite in His sight." Eli listened, the initial flicker of misunderstanding dawning slowly into clarity. He had seen many who came to the tabernacle bearing petitions, but this woman's plea held an uncommon fire — a mixture of desperation and unwavering faith. Yet, in the priest's mind, there was a shadow of doubt, born from years of watching hope transformed into disappointment. "Woman," Eli said solemnly, "may you find favor in the eyes of the Lord. Go in peace, and may the God of Israel grant your prayer. Let your vow be made known and fulfilled." The blessing came with a weighty gravity that seemed to still the very air, as if the tabernacle itself acknowledged the profound exchange unfolding within its sacred precincts. Hannah felt it—the tremor in her soul that heralded divine assurance, the quiet confirmation that her petition had taken root in the heavens. "Thank you, my lord," she whispered, tears glistening in her eyes. "Your words have lifted the burden from my soul. May the God whom you serve bless you in return." Eli nodded, a faint smile breaking through the creases of his weathered face. "Go in peace, and may the God of Abraham, Isaac, and Jacob walk beside you always." The tabernacle seemed to breathe with reverence around them, the flickering lamps bowing before the weight of Hannah's sacred promise. The ancient stones, steeped in centuries of worship and divine encounter, held witness to this humble woman's sacred vow—a moment that would ripple through Israel's history. This encounter was not merely a meeting of two souls within a holy place; it was a convergence of human yearning and divine purpose, a threshold upon which God's plan began to unfold. The temple, with its priestly rituals and sacred customs, served as the stage for this sacred dialogue—a place where the broken found voice and the impossible found possibility. Historically, the role of the high priest was far more than ceremonial. Eli, descendant of Aaron's line, bore the heavy mantle of mediator between Israel and her God. He was entrusted with supervising the sacrificial system, maintaining the tabernacle's sanctity, and instructing the people in Torah. His duties extended into the spiritual realm, where his intercession carried the hopes and fears of a nation. Yet, like all men, Eli was fallible, caught in the tension between divine command and human weakness. In the world of temple worship, the sanctity of space and time was paramount. The flickering lamps illuminated not just the stone and wood but the mystery of God's presence dwelling in the midst of His people. The rituals performed, from offering sacrifices to burning incense, signified Israel's acknowledgment of dependence on the divine. Hannah's presence here, unadorned and vulnerable, underscored the intimate intersection between the sacred and the personal. Her vow was distinct in its nature and profound in consequence—the offering of a child as a Nazirite bound by lifelong dedication to God. Nazirites were consecrated individuals, set apart through abstinence and purity as signs of special devotion (Numbers 6). By pledging her unborn son to this sacred calling, Hannah entered into a covenant that transcended human desire. It was a testament of faith bridging human frailty with divine faithfulness. Eli's blessing thus carried dual significance: an acknowledgment of Hannah's faith and an invocation of God's power to fulfill promises through unexpected means. His ministry within the temple had prepared him to recognize the sacredness of such encounters—the moments when God stirred among His people through their surrender and hope. As Hannah departed the tabernacle, her steps lighter though her burden remained, the seeds of destiny had been sown in the quiet depths of the night. The interplay of fear, hope, and holy resolve wove a tapestry that would shape the narrative of a nation. The destiny of Samuel was born not merely from the hands of mortals but within the sacred embrace of a covenant forged under flickering lamps and the watchful eyes of a fading high priest. This meeting between Hannah and Eli encapsulates the profound theological truth that divine grace often reveals itself in human weakness and vulnerability. It highlights the priestly role as both intercessor and witness to God's unfolding plan, while also demonstrating the power of faith-filled vows within Israel's religious tradition. It is a pivotal moment linking the personal agony of infertility with the grand narrative of covenant fulfillment, a bridge between the private supplicant and the public servant. In reflecting upon this encounter, one cannot separate the spiritual atmosphere from the cultural and historical realities of Israelite worship. The tabernacle was not merely a backdrop but a dynamic participant in this sacred drama. It was a living symbol of God's dwelling among His people—a place where heaven touched earth and where hope was kindled in the hearts of the faithful. The promise made in that dim sanctuary echoed beyond the stones and smoke, asserting the truth that God's timing and purposes would prevail. For Hannah, it was the genesis of a new chapter, one that would bring forth a prophet destined to alter the course of Israel's history. For Eli, it was a moment of grace amid the twilight of his own priestly career, offering a glimpse of renewal and divine intervention. Such an encounter resonates deeply even now, inviting readers into the timeless interplay of human longing and divine response. It reminds us that within the quiet corners of faith, amid whispered prayers and sacred promises, the threads of destiny are woven with care — and that the God who hears is ever faithful to fulfill His word. This spiritual encounter stands as a testament to the enduring power of hope and the transformative potential of sacred vows. It also reveals the profound importance of the priestly office in Israel, serving as the vital link between God and His people. Eli's blessing, born from both tradition and divine insight, affirmed that within the dim recesses of the tabernacle, God's plan was taking shape—one that would ripple through generations and redefine the nation's destiny. The encounter of Hannah and Eli thus captures a moment suspended between earth and heaven, between supplication and promise, between mystery and revelation. It invites us to witness the sacred dialogue where a barren woman's tears meet the priest's steady blessing, creating the beginning of a story that would echo across centuries and continue to inspire faith, hope, and devotion. Such is the enduring legacy of that night within the tabernacle—the place where a humble vow met a priest's blessing, wrapped in shadows, flame, and the ever-present silence of God's listening heart.

Birth and Blessing Under Desert Stars

Beneath a vast canopy of desert stars, the world seemed hushed, as if holding its breath in reverence for the moment that was to unfold. The cool night air whispered softly through the olive groves, carrying with it the scent of earth warmed by day and the faint aroma of wild thyme. Crickets sang their steady chorus, punctuated only by the gentle rustling of palm leaves swaying in the evening breeze. In the stillness of this rural expanse, far from the bustling city and the sounds of the world's clamor, life awaited a miracle—a child who would mark a turning point in the unfolding story of Israel. At the edge of the village, where stone homes clustered around the altar of faith that was the Tabernacle, a woman stood beneath the shimmering stars, her soul a tapestry woven from longing, devotion, and quiet hope. Hannah, a name whispered with both pain and prayer throughout the years, cradled the promise of a future blessed by God's mercy in her heart. Her journey had been long and arduous; years of barrenness etched deep lines of sorrow upon her face. Yet tonight, under this suspended sky, those lines softened into the gentle glow of a mother's joy, her very being radiant with the fulfillment of a vow made in sacred desperation. The dawn of Samuel's life was not heralded by trumpets or fanfare, but by the profound silence of the desert night, a silence pregnant with possibility. It was within this sacred stillness that Hannah's prayer was answered, her burdens mysteriously lifted, and a son born who would carry the weight of a nation upon his shoulders. This birth did not merely mark the coming of a child; it signaled the dawn of a new covenant between God and His people, woven intricately into the tapestry of faith, sacrifice, and destiny. Hannah's humble dwelling, modest yet filled with the warmth of her spirit, bore witness to the quiet unfolding of Samuel's earliest breaths. The soft murmur of her prayers merged with the gentle breath of the infant, each sound a sacred melody echoing beneath the eternal stars. Outside, village life stirred faintly in the distance—the low murmur of women caring for other children, the occasional bark of a dog, the subdued movement of those who respected the night's sanctity. All seemed touched by the sacredness of this moment, as if the very earth held its breath to witness the miracle of new life blessed by divine grace. In the weeks that followed, the desert night remained a silent guardian over the infant Samuel. His cries blended with the songs of the night, the tender lullabies hummed by his mother becoming a prayer woven with love and resolve. Hannah's heart was filled with a sacred promise, made palpable through the simple yet profound act of holding her son close. Every smile, every flutter of small fists, every stretch of his tiny limbs echoed a divine covenant—a pledge that he was set apart, destined to be a vessel of God's will in a time that would shape the future of Israel. The narrative of Samuel's birth unfolds like the gentle blooming of a desert flower—slow, deliberate, and imbued with delicate beauty. Each moment pulses with the rhythm of life's renewal, a tender reminder that within the vast wilderness of human longing and divine intention, hope takes root beneath the most arid of skies. Hannah's joy was tempered by a solemn awareness; her son was no ordinary child but a sacred gift entrusted to her by God, one destined to serve beyond the bounds of ordinary existence. As the stars wheeled overhead, casting their silver light upon the earth, Hannah's thoughts reached beyond her humble home to the Tabernacle's sacred precincts. There, the presence of the Lord was felt not only in the flickering flames of the altar but in the whispered prayers of a nation yearning for deliverance. She knew her pledge must now be fulfilled—that Samuel would be dedicated wholly to God's service, set apart from the world to walk a path of divine purpose and profound challenge. This act of surrender was not easy; it was the very essence of sacrifice, a mother's love willing to release her child into the hands of the Almighty. Surrendering Samuel to the care of Eli, the aged priest whose wise eyes held the weight of years and the burden of a priesthood in decline, was an act steeped in faith and solemnity. Hannah's heart trembled with both sorrow and hope as she watched her son taken to dwell in the Tabernacle's hallowed halls. Yet even in release, there was an unbreakable bond—a sacred tether woven from love and unyielding trust in the God who had answered prayers beneath the desert stars. The desert nights continued to bear witness to this sacred exchange—the mother's whispered blessings mingling with the priest's prayers, the solemn incantations of faith rising like incense into the eternal night. Samuel's earliest days were steeped not only in human care but in the profound presence of the divine. The land, the stars, the soft desert breeze—each seemed to converge in this hallowed moment, enfolding the infant prophet in the mystery of a destiny that would ripple through generations. Within this silent, sacred space, themes of sacrifice and destiny intertwined seamlessly. Hannah's dedication was both a relinquishing and a reclaiming—a recognition that the child she bore was a gift not merely to her but to the entire community of Israel. This act embodied the paradox at the heart of the human-divine relationship: surrender that brings blessing, loss that uncovers purpose, endings that herald beginnings. Through these tender moments, the reader glimpses the profound truth that Samuel's life was irrevocably bound to a higher calling, marked by the quiet radiance of faith made flesh. Though Samuel's birth was a singular event, the echoes of that moment stretched far beyond the humble dwelling beneath the desert sky. The stillness of the night resonated with the unfurling of a story much larger than any one family—an epic of divine intervention, human courage, and the unfolding promise of hope in a time shadowed by uncertainty. The boy who cried out beneath the stars was a beacon born into a world poised on the cusp of transformation, a world eager for the voice that would one day usher Israel out of chaos and into covenantal renewal. The soft night breezes carried the promise of that future, rustling the olive branches like whispered prayers from the earth itself. Village life, with all its simple joys and struggles, pulsed faintly beneath the celestial dome, a reminder that even the smallest moments are touched by the divine hand. Within Hannah's embrace, the infant Samuel lay quiet and still, a testament to the mysterious ways in which God works—through silence and sound, through hope and sacrifice, through the tender intertwining of human hearts and holy purpose. As the dawn slowly broke, scattering gold across the desert sands and painting the horizon with hues of rose and amber, the birth of Samuel stood as a beacon of new beginnings. It was a birth that spoke not only of life itself but of a mission transcending time—a mission birthed in shadows yet destined to illumine the path ahead. The stars that watched over his coming faded gently into the morning light, yet their silent witness lingered on, etched into the very fabric of history, faith, and the human spirit. Thus, from the quiet soil of a desert night, a prophet arose—shaped by the divine promise cradled in his mother's heart and the blessing granted beneath the desert stars. His journey began in whispered prayers and steadfast faith, a journey that would etch his name across the annals of Israel with the indelible ink of destiny. Through the tender moments of his earliest days, the story of Samuel's birth reveals the delicate dance between human longing and divine will, a dance played out beneath the eternal heavens where hope and sacrifice were woven tightly together in the loom of destiny.

In the Shadow of Eli: Childhood Among the Priests

Life Within the Sanctuary Walls

The sanctuary was a world apart from the ordinary realm of childhood—a sacred enclave where the air seemed thick with the weight of ancient prayers and the flickering glow of oil lamps cast long, dancing shadows upon stone and wood. Within these holy walls, Samuel's earliest memories took root: the faint scent of burning incense, the steady rhythm of his footsteps reverberating on the worn earthen floor, and the low murmur of the Levitical priests as they moved about their solemn tasks. It was beneath the watchful eye of Eli, the high priest, that Samuel's boyhood unfolded — a life shaped not by playful freedom or carefree leisure, but by the austere discipline and profound spirituality of the tabernacle. Each morning, as the first pale light of dawn crept over the plains of Shiloh, Samuel awoke to the muffled calls of the temple priests beginning their day. The sanctity of the tabernacle imposed a rhythm distinct from that of children growing up elsewhere. There was no leisurely rising or the uproar of neighborhood games; instead, his day was ushered in with the reverent clatter of priestly garments and the rustle of sacred scrolls. From the moment he opened his eyes, Samuel's senses were immersed in the sanctuary's solemn cadence. The young boy's quarters were modest, carved from the simple stone buildings clustered near the sanctuary's outer courts. His lodgings were a place of quiet austerity, barren but for the essentials—an unadorned cot, a rough woven blanket, and a small table upon which rested a few everyday objects: a wooden bowl for washing, a lamp filled with olive oil, and a clay jar of fresh water. A faint, persistent aroma lingered here—of smoke mingled with cedarwood and the waxy residue of the many lamps, giving the room a permanence that spoke of years spent in prayer and service. Yet within this stark environment, Samuel's world held a strange vitality. The sanctuary was alive with sounds both sacred and mundane, weaving together to form the backdrop of his childhood. The steady chant of the morning psalms rose and fell like waves breaking against the stone walls. The clinking of priestly utensils—silver basins, bronze censers, and sacrificial knives—provided a metallic counterpoint to the murmured recitations of the Levitical priests. Occasionally, Eli's booming voice would ring out from the inner sanctum, addressing his sons or instructing Samuel on matters of temple protocol and ancient law. Samuel's days followed a strict regimen, one that melded the practical with the spiritual. Before the sun fully warmed the air, he would accompany one of the younger priests to draw fresh water from the well—clear and cold, its surface broken by the rhythmic splash of a wooden bucket. With water in hand, they would cleanse the altar—a sacred duty involving the removal of ashes and the careful arrangement of fresh wood for sacrifices. The smell of burning cedar and frankincense would soon follow, filling the sanctuary with a heady fragrance that seemed to sanctify both stone and soul. Though he was still a boy, Samuel was given responsibilities not unlike those carried out by men twice his age. Under Eli's watchful guidance, he learned to prepare the sacred vessels, arrange the sacrifices, and tend to the lamps that burned continually before the Holy Place. These were not simple chores but acts steeped in meaning, each step a link in a chain that connected the present moment to the covenant between God and Israel. Samuel performed these duties with a mixture of awe and determination; he was aware, even in his youth, that his service was a form of worship, a way to draw closer to the God whose presence hovered invisibly within the tabernacle's curtained walls. The architecture of the sanctuary itself reinforced the weight of Samuel's upbringing. The courtyard, enclosed by linen hangings and wooden pillars, was where daily sacrifices took place—the cries of burnt offerings mingling with the low prayers of worshippers who gathered to present their gifts. Beyond lay the Holy Place, a small chamber harboring the table of showbread, the golden lampstand, and the altar of incense. Further still, behind a thick veil, lay the Most Holy Place—the inner sanctum where the Ark of the Covenant rested, surrounded by cherubim of gold. Samuel's knowledge of these sacred spaces was more than academic; they were places he grieved to approach and revered to the utmost, for they symbolized the very dwelling of God among His people. The contrast between Samuel's innocence and the gravity of this religious environment was stark. While other children roamed fields or sailed small boats on nearby streams, Samuel's playground was shaped by divine presence and ritual obligation. Yet this was no sterile solitude. The boy's interactions with the priests and with Eli himself nurtured a seedbed of spiritual formation. Eli, despite his advancing years and his own familial struggles, was a figure of paternal authority and religious wisdom. To Samuel, he was both mentor and guardian, imparting lessons not only about ritual purity but about discerning the voice of God amidst the clamor of life. As days turned into weeks, Samuel's spiritual sensitivity grew more discernible. His dreams were often vivid, filled with strange images and voices that stirred his young heart. Sometimes, in the hush of the night, when the tabernacle lay bathed in moonlight and the stillness pressed upon the ancient stones, Samuel felt a presence that was neither sight nor sound but a living weight upon his soul. It was a stirring neither he nor Eli could wholly explain, yet it hinted at a calling beyond mere servitude—a divine summons that would one day alter the course of Israel's history. Within these sanctuary walls, Samuel also witnessed the imperfections and failings of those tasked with holiness. He observed the shortcomings of Eli's sons—Hophni and Phinehas—whose corruption cast a shadow over the priestly line. Their greed and disregard for the sacrificial laws underscored the heavy cost of spiritual neglect. For the boy, these encounters were lessons in the complexities of faith and leadership, teaching him that devotion was neither simple nor guaranteed by virtue of birthright. Despite these challenges, the tabernacle remained a place of profound hope and sacred mystery. The daily rituals, repeated in measured routine, were moments where time itself seemed to pause. The lighting of lamps, the kindling of incense, the careful arrangement of bread—all reflected a divine order, a cosmic rhythm in which Samuel found his place. It was as though each act of devotion formed part of a tapestry, weaving human humility with divine grace.Samuel's relationship with the sanctuary was deeply formative, shaping both his character and his future prophetic vocation. The lessons of discipline, reverence, and vigilance imprinted upon his soul a capacity for hearing and discerning God's voice. The sacred environment taught him patience and humility, for the altar did not bend to human will, and the mysteries of the Most Holy Place remained veiled. Yet it was here, in this paradox of concealment and revelation, that Samuel began to understand his unique role as mediator between God and Israel. In the quiet evenings, after the day's work was done and the priests withdrew from the inner courts, Samuel would sit alone in the dim glow of a single lamp, pondering the scriptures and the stories handed down through the generations. These moments of solitude were his refuge—a space for reflection and prayer. The boundary between boy and prophet blurred in these hours; his thoughts were filled with questions about God's justice, mercy, and the future of his people. Occasionally, pilgrims would arrive from distant tribes, bringing offerings and seeking counsel. Samuel listened attentively to their stories and petitions, gaining an early understanding of Israel's hopes and fears. In their supplications, he glimpsed the burdens that faith placed upon the community, as well as the longing for a leader who could guide them through turbulent times. These encounters sealed within him a rising sense of responsibility, even as he remained but a boy in the shadow of Eli. The sanctuary was not just a physical space but a crucible of transformation. Within its walls, Samuel's identity was forged through the interplay of innocence and experience, obedience and revelation. Each day spent among the sacred vessels, the lampstands, and the stone altars deepened his comprehension of holiness—not as a distant ideal but a living reality demanding commitment and courage. Through years of steadfast dedication, Samuel's boyhood became inexorably linked with the sanctuary's eternal purpose. The delicate balance of childlike wonder and sober responsibility nurtured a heart attuned to God's will. It was within this hallowed precinct that Samuel learned to listen—not only to the words of men but to the silent voice that would one day call him to stand as Israel's prophet, judge, and kingmaker. In those formative years, surrounded by torchlight flickering against the weathered stones, by prayers echoing toward the heavens, and by the unyielding presence of God's covenant, Samuel's journey began—a journey that would shape a nation and resonate through history. The sanctuary walls, austere yet sacred, held the secrets of a boy on the cusp of destiny, preparing him for the monumental tasks that lay ahead. Thus, life within the sanctuary was more than mere existence: it was the cradle of divine purpose, the forge of prophetic vision, and the foundation of a legacy that would endure long after the flickering lamps had burned low and silence had reclaimed the tabernacle's ancient stones.

Eli's Burdened Eyes

The flickering candlelight cast long, wavering shadows on the worn walls of the sanctuary, and within those shadows stood Eli, a man whose eyes told a tale of burdens far heavier than age alone could explain. His gaze, once sharp and commanding as the high priest of Israel, had settled into a glaze of weariness—a gaze tethered to a lifetime of sacred duties, personal losses, and the slow collapse of the spiritual order he had pledged to uphold. To the world, Eli was a venerable figure, a bridge between divine will and the people of Israel; but beneath the weight of his priestly robes beat the heart of a man beleaguered by sorrows deep and unresolved. Eli's days now dragged in a twilight between memory and desperation. Each morning, he awoke not with renewed strength, but with the creaking ache of bones betraying time's relentless march and a spirit gnawed by doubts that prayer alone could not assuage. The elders and priests sought his counsel; the people looked up to him as an intermediary to Yahweh. Yet inside, Eli grappled with a gnawing sense of failure—a failure rooted not merely in his advancing years but in his inability to steer his own household away from ruin. His sons, Hophni and Phinehas, had stained the priesthood with their corruption, turning what should have been hallowed duties into acts of greed, lust, and sacrilege. Their misdeeds were whispered in hushed tones throughout Shiloh, eroding the trust of the people and sullying the altar's sanctity. Eli knew of their transgressions, felt the pangs of agony with every tale that reached his ears, yet he was shackled by a complex web of paternal love, spiritual responsibility, and perhaps a measure of denial. Sitting low on the bench by the side of the sanctuary, Eli's hands folded before him, the rough calluses on his palms echoed decades of labor and ritual. He closed his eyes, seeking solace in prayer, but his mind wandered—caught in the relentless tempest of what-ifs and yet-to-be. He thought of his youth, the days when the ark still journeyed with their people, when leaders rose and fell, but faith remained unshaken. He remembered the laughter of his sons as boys, innocent and hopeful, before the dark paths they now trod." How long, Lord, how long?" he whispered into the silence. The sanctuary was quiet except for the soft groans of the wind outside, rustling the trees and rattling the shutters. It was here, in this fragile stillness, that Eli wrestled with his own reflection. An old man, yes, but more profoundly, a man broken by the weight of legacy. His eyes traced the carved wood of the altar, each notch a testament to years of sacrifice and covenant. And yet, the altar now seemed more a relic than a promise—a monument to a past rapidly dissolving into chaos. His sons—how had they fallen so far? Eli recalled how they had been raised in the very shadow of the sanctuary, apprentices to their father's sacred office. Their mouths were trained to speak the words of the Lord; their hands groomed to offer the sacrifices in the prescribed manner. Yet power, it seemed, had poisoned their hearts. They took from the people more than was their due, and mocked the sacrifices without reverence. Stories reached even Eli's ears of them taking the choicest portions from the offerings, both offering the Lord's people a corrupted faith, and themselves defiling the holy ground they were charged to guard. When confronted, they scorned him with brazen contempt. Perhaps it was the weariness in his voice or the slow decline in his vigor that sapped his ability to discipline them adequately. Yet every corrective word felt like a fracture in the foundation of family, every rebuke a widening chasm between father and sons. The burden tore at him, for Eli's heart was a house divided—between his roles as priest and judge and as a father. And the conflict gnawed at the edges of his soul, fraying the very fabric of his faith. At times, Eli's eyes filled with tears that would never be seen. Tears not only for his errant sons but for the people of Israel, whose faith was faltering as the priesthood's integrity crumbled. He knew well the words of the prophets that warned of the decay of leaders and the consequences of a shepherd who misled the flock. The sanctity of the covenant was threatened, and Eli stood powerless before the rising tide of corruption. Yet amidst the darkness, a fragile light remained: a quiet hope wrapped in the innocence of a child named Samuel. The boy was placed under his care, a child dedicated by Hannah in a prayerful plea for divine favor. Samuel's presence stirred something long dormant within Eli's spirit—a glimmer of renewal, a tentative promise whispered by the divine itself, that restoration was still possible. When Samuel first arrived, a shadow of doubt crossed Eli's heart. Could this child, growing within the very walls once tainted by Hophni and Phinehas, truly herald a new dawn? Could his purity and devotion fortify a priesthood weary and wayward? And yet, as Eli began to watch the boy, the answers slowly unfurled like the dawn breaking through a murky night. Samuel listened closely, his eyes wide and attentive, his hands steady and respectful when learning the sacred rites. Unlike Eli's sons, Samuel's presence did not stir quarreling or dishonor but brought with it a quiet reverence that seemed to pull the cornerstones of Eli's world back into alignment. Watching the boy was both balm and burden—the reminder of what had been lost, and the fragile hope of what might yet be. Sleep came little to Eli these days, and often found him lingering by the temple's outer walls, staring into the darkened landscape, as if searching for answers amid the stars. The silence of the night was both companion and judge, forcing Eli to confront the void between who he was and who he wished to be. In the solitude, the godly burdens upon his shoulders pressed down with unrelenting weight—the fear that his family's sins would bring about divine judgment, the sorrow of witnessing a nation's faith erode, and the despair of feeling ill-equipped to guide the people as their spiritual shepherd. Though his body fragile, Eli's spirit wrestled fiercely with the concept of justice and mercy, punishment and forgiveness. Deep within, he sensed the encroaching shadow of divine retribution—that the Lord's patience had its limits—but he also longed for redemption, for a miracle to restore the priesthood's honor and revive Israel's trust. This conflicted landscape of hope and fear carved deep lines into his face, aged him beyond the tally of years, and filled his eyes with a somber knowledge few could understand. Eli's burden was not simply the struggle against his sons' wickedness, nor the frustration over a generation's apostasy, but the intimate anguish of a man torn between worlds. He was a priest serving a holy God, beholden to law and tradition, yet also a father whose heart broke at the failings within his own household. This duality left him vulnerable, prone to moments of despair interlaced with fierce resolve. One afternoon, as the sun cast a bleak orange glow across the barren hills around Shiloh, Eli sat beside the spring where the priests gathered to wash before service. The cool water reflected his lined face, heavy with the weight of judgment deferred and hope deferred still. His voice, when he finally broke the silence, carried a quiet, aching lament." How long will my sons mock the altar? How long will my people's hearts be hardened? Where is the mercy in the land when the sanctuary groans beneath unholy hands?" His hands clenched the edge of the basin, knuckles white with the force of unspoken prayers and unanswered questions. The land around him was open, yet Eli felt enclosed—trapped within the confines of a legacy slipping through his fingers like sand. The voices around him murmured of impending doom, of the Lord's hand poised to bring swift justice. And yet, even amidst such certainty of downfall, Eli held to what remained — Samuel, the flickering flame of promise in a temple grown cold. The boy's innocence was a balm to Eli's frayed soul. In Samuel, Eli saw not just a pupil but a covenant forged anew—a chance for correction and healing beyond the shadow of corruption. He took the boy under his guidance, teaching him the sacred rites and opening his ears to the whispers of the divine. With patience born of years baptized in both joy and grief, Eli sought to nurture Samuel's spirit, aware that the boy's path might diverge from his own faded journey. Still, even as Eli invested hope in Samuel, the shadows of his sons' sins loomed large. The community's confidence eroded daily, priests squabbled for a share of sacrifices they had no right to claim, and the cloud of judgment hung heavy and inevitable. Eli's heart ached, torn between protecting the boy entrusted to him and the knowledge that the day of reckoning for his household drew near. One evening, in the solitude of his chamber, Eli's reflections plunged him into a tempest of conflicting emotions. His heart was heavy with sorrow and shame, yet a quiet resolve whispered to rise above the failures and place trust in the divine. The stillness was broken by a sudden flicker of remembered words from the elders—the prophecy announcing the fall of Eli's house, a stark declaration that the sins of the father would be visited upon the sons, and that the tabernacle would soon be left desolate. Eli's eyes flooded with tears, the first in many months, as he grappled with the looming fate foretold by divine revelation. This was not simply the death knell of a family line, but a decisive moment marking the end of an era in Israel's spiritual history—a moment that would usher in the transition from the judges to the kings, a shift so profound that the weight of it crushed even the eldest priest's weary soul. Yet in this breaking dawn, Eli found a measure of peace. He understood that his role, though fraught with pain, was part of a divine tapestry larger than his own missteps and regrets. His guidance of Samuel was not a mere task but a bridge toward a new beginning, a handing over of the torch from faded strength to youthful vigor. Even as his body sagged and his eyes clouded with the passage of time, Eli's spirit remained vigilant, enduring the darkest nights with a quiet strength born of faithful service. He bore his burdens openly in the silence of prayer, wrestling with the tension between despair and hope, corruption and renewal. The days moved slowly for Eli, each one a testament to survival amid the encroaching twilight. His watchful eyes remained fixed on the boy Samuel, the embodiment of divine promise amid human frailty. And as the fires of his sons' corruption blazed out, threatening to consume all that he had held sacred, Eli's burdened eyes looked beyond the horizon—toward the faint, growing light of a new era poised to rise from the ashes of past failures. Eli's story is not merely one of decline and despair, but of enduring faith in the face of loss; a portrait of a man transformed by the anguish of his own limitations, steadfast in the knowledge that even the darkest night must yield to dawn. It is through Eli's vision—the burdened eyes that see both the sins of the present and the hope of the future—that the legacy of Samuel begins to unfold, forever entwined with the fate of Israel itself.

The Stirring Call Within

In the dim recesses of the ancient tabernacle, amidst the flickering shadows cast by oil lamps, the boy Samuel began to awaken to a whispering presence that was at once intimate and vast. The holy sanctuary, a place of solemn mystery and awe, had been his home since infancy—his earliest memories entwined with the murmurs of sacred texts and the fragrant embrace of incense smoke. Yet, it was only now, in the delicate threshold of adolescence, that Samuel sensed an unfolding within himself, a subtle stirring that beckoned him beyond the familiar rhythms of priestly duty and the watchful eyes of Eli. These early years were marked by a peculiar blend of contrasts. On one hand, the sanctuary was a realm filled with sacred traditions, nightly sacrifices, and the solemn steps of the priests who ministered before the Lord; on the other, a vulnerable witness to human failings, political intrigue, and moral shadows lurking beyond the altar's glow. Samuel's world was poised precariously between light and darkness—a crucible in which the seeds of his prophetic vocation were quietly germinating. The nights held a sacred stillness, punctuated only by the occasional creak of wood or the soft shuffle of sandals on stone floors. In these moments, Samuel would lie awake on his rough mat within the priests' quarters, the coolness of the room mingling with the faint scent of burnt offerings. His ears tuned to the silence, his breath steady but his heart restless, he began to feel an inexplicable presence pressing close, subtle as a breeze slipping through the curtain of the Most Holy Place. It was during such moments that the divine call first brushed against the edges of his consciousness. Not like a thunderous proclamation, but as something tender yet compelling—an almost imperceptible voice whispering his name in the quiet dark. At first, he imagined it was Eli, calling him to some task or to rise and pray. Yet the echo of that voice was different, unfamiliar, and deeply gentle, commanding attention through a bond that transcended mere words." Samuel... Samuel." The name echoed within his soul, stirring a blend of wonder and fear. To respond was to acknowledge a reality greater than himself—a reality that would eventually require courage to embrace. Yet, the boy was hesitant, uncertain whether he was yet worthy or prepared to heed such a summons. The feeling was akin to standing at the edge of a vast forest, where the path forward was shrouded in mist, beckoning but unknown. Within the priestly quarters under Eli's watchful gaze, Samuel navigated the tender age between boyhood and manhood, absorbing lessons not only in ritual and scripture but in the harsh truths of human nature. Eli, though aged and burdened, offered a model of steadfast devotion, his hands worn by decades of sacrificial service. Yet even Eli's venerable presence could not mask the corruption growing in the temple—the sons of Eli, Hophni and Phinehas, whose reckless indulgence and abuse of sacred duties cast a long shadow over the sanctuary's holiness. Samuel observed these failings with a sorrowful clarity rare for one so young. Unlike the careless arrogance of Eli's sons, he possessed a reverence that was both natural and deepening with each passing day. In his quiet moments by the altar, surrounded by the gentle glow of the lampstand and the soft rustle of the curtains, Samuel wrestled with a growing awareness of responsibility—a call to righteousness amid the rising tide of impiety. His spiritual sensitivity manifested not only in moments of prayer but in subtle, almost mystical experiences. Sometimes, in the solitude of pre-dawn hours, when the first light stretched pale fingers across the horizon, and the temple was steeped in stillness, Samuel would feel a warm, enveloping presence—an embrace not of flesh, but of spirit. The sensation was at once comforting and humbling; it seemed to reassure the boy that his path was watched over, even if the way was uncertain. At other times, vivid dreams would grip him. These dreams were not the fanciful images of childhood, but mysterious visions that lingered at the borders of understanding—a tapestry of glimpses hinting at the destiny awaiting him and the fate of Israel itself. In these nocturnal visitations, Samuel stood beneath a sky ablaze with countless stars, or heard the weeping cries of a nation in turmoil, or saw the silhouette of a man anointed with oil, destined to lead his people. Though the full meaning eluded him, an unseen force urged him to prepare—to listen and to wait. When the voice called again, persistent and clear in the darkness, it stirred within Samuel a learning of sacred patience. At first, he ran to Eli, believing the old priest was the source of the summons. "Here I am," he said, rising quickly from his bed. But Eli would answer, "I did not call you; lie down again." This happened three times, each occasion deepening the boy's confusion and solemnity. Only after the third call did Eli comprehend that the Lord was speaking directly to Samuel. Gently, he instructed the boy on how to respond: "If He calls you again, say, 'Speak, Lord, for Your servant is listening." The simple words held profound significance, marking a pivotal moment in Samuel's life—the conscious acceptance of his role as a servant not merely to the priesthood but to God himself. It was an opening of the heart, a surrender to the divine will that would shape his identity and mission forever. The atmosphere within the tabernacle was thick with tension during these days. The priestly sons' misdeeds had begun to alienate the people, who murmured discontentedly beyond the camp's outer tents. The sacred place, once a beacon of hope and covenant, now seemed vulnerable to decay. Against this backdrop, Samuel's emerging vocation felt like a fragile flame in a storm—steady, yet requiring careful nurturing. In the face of this delicate balance, Samuel exhibited an innocence unblemished by cynicism but tempered by early confrontation with human frailty. His youth was a canvas on which the morning light of

God's calling was gradually painted, layering purity with an increasing awareness of destiny's weight. As days grew into weeks, Samuel's role within the tabernacle subtly shifted. The priests began to entrust him with more responsibilities—not mere menial tasks but those requiring careful attention to ritual detail and the maintenance of holiness. This trust, born from Samuel's steadfast character and reverence, further differentiated him from the corrupt sons of Eli and the other temple attendants. His sense of purpose grew in tandem with the tasks he performed, each offering a tangible connection to the divine presence he felt stirring within. Language learned from scripture and from Eli's teachings seeped into Samuel's consciousness, embedding holy truths and prophetic imagery: the Holy One of Israel, the Lord who hears, the righteous Judge, the Shepherd-King. These titles were not abstract concepts but living realities that beckoned Samuel to a role that transcended youth and enforced expectations. They spoke of a leadership not grounded in earthly power but in divine authority and moral integrity. Yet, this was no easy path. Samuel's adolescence was punctuated by moments of doubt and loneliness. The knowledge of the sacred burden resting on his shoulders was both a blessing and a heavy cross. Often, he would retreat to the mountain slopes beyond the camp, where the whispering wind and ancient trees provided a silent audience for his prayers and ponderings. Here, the boy wrestled with the tension between duty and desire—the longing for a simple life and the inexorable call to purpose. The divine stirrings within Samuel's heart were accompanied by an increasing sensitivity to his surroundings. He could intuit the distress of the people, the tremors of fear and rebellion that pulsed through the camp. The sacred space itself seemed to echo with unspoken laments and warnings, as if the very stones bore witness to a coming upheaval. In this heightened awareness, Samuel learned to hear not only the Lord's voice but also the cries of a nation on the cusp of transformation. His relationship with Eli deepened during this period, marked by moments of teaching and silent mentorship. Though Eli was burdened by grief and the failings of his sons, his faith remained a guiding light. He shared with

Samuel the ancient stories of the patriarchs, the promises made to Abraham, Isaac, and

Jacob—stories that held the key to understanding Israel's identity and future promise. Through these narratives, Samuel absorbed a vision of God's unwavering faithfulness, even amid human frailty. Yet, alongside hope, there was a palpable sense of impending change. Eli would often warn Samuel of the consequences of disobedience and the impending judgment that might befall the house of the Lord. These sobering lessons echoed in Samuel's heart, cultivating a reverence for God's justice that would characterize his later prophetic ministry. One quiet morning, just as the sun's first rays pierced the eastern sky, Samuel found himself standing alone before the altar. The air was cool, the scent of burnt offering still lingering. In the silence, he lifted a simple prayer, a whispered petition born of both youthful longing and deep faith. "Lord, what is Your will for me? How shall I serve You?" In that moment, a stillness settled over the sanctuary, profound and assuring. Samuel felt a warmth flow through him, a confirmation that his life was indeed bound to a holy purpose. Though he did not yet understand all the details, the seed had been firmly planted. He was to be a prophet—a messenger, a guide, a voice for the people of Israel. This realization transformed Samuel's inner world. The tug of the divine call was no longer a distant murmur but a vital presence shaping his daily existence. With it came a dawning maturity—not only spiritual but emotional and intellectual. The boy who had once simply served now carried the mark of one chosen to lead, to confront injustice, and to speak truth, even when it was difficult. Through the years that followed, Samuel's spiritual sensitivity continued to blossom. The Lord's voice became a familiar melody, guiding his decisions and fortifying his resolve. His adolescence, shadowed by the failings within the priesthood, became a crucible, forging in him an unshakable commitment to righteousness and covenant fidelity. In the soft interplay between innocence and responsibility, Samuel's character was being etched with divine precision. The delicate balance he maintained—as a boy aware of both his limitations and his calling—would define his role in Israel's history as no other prophet before or after. The story of Samuel's stirring call within is not simply an account of youthful awakening but an invitation to witness the sacred moment when God's voice intersects with human heart. It is the moment when a boy, surrounded by the frailty and corruption of his world, chooses to listen—and in that listening, finds a destiny that will shape a nation.

Corruption and Consequence

The sanctuary at Shiloh, once a beacon of divine presence and national hope, had become a place where the glow of holiness flickered uncertainly beneath the weight of neglect and moral decay. In the shadows of its sacred courts, the priesthood—the very custodians of Israel's covenant with Yahweh—were slipping into corruption, their stewardship tainted by greed and lust. This was an era not only of religious laxity but of profound cultural disintegration, setting the stage for a reckoning that would ripple through the entire nation. At the heart of this crisis stood Eli, the venerable high priest and judge, a man of great age and declining vision, whose weaknesses compounded the ruin around him. Eli was caught between his loyalty to his sons and his duty to God and Israel—a tension that ultimately yielded tragic consequences. His sons, Hophni and Phinehas, men who ought to have exemplified priestly virtue and obedience, instead became the embodiment of sacrilege and abuse of power. Their actions would bring to bear divine judgement and alter the course not only of their family but of the Israelite people themselves. The days and nights within the precincts of the Tabernacle at Shiloh played out as a stark dichotomy. The rituals, sacrifices, and feasts that once united the people in shared worship against a backdrop of covenant faithfulness unfolded alongside a hidden darkness—a shadow cast by the very men charged with guarding God's holiness. These contradictory realities—the outward celebration of tradition and the inner corruption of spirit—paint a vivid tableau of Israel's unfolding crisis. The sons of Eli wielded their priestly privileges like weapons rather than sacred trusts. Instead of serving the Lord sincerely and ministering justly to the people, they exploited their positions to satisfy selfish desires. They took for themselves the best portions of the sacrifices—the fat and choice meat that by divine law belonged to them under the covenant—but did so with greed and ruthlessness, refusing to give the people their due portions in a manner marked by respect and reverence for the sacrificial system. Their disdain extended beyond mere gluttony; they exhibited blatant disrespect for the worshippers, behaving arrogantly and shamelessly. Worse still was their treatment of the women who served at the sanctuary. Scripture and tradition tell us that a number of female attendants ministered within Shiloh's sacred space, assisting with various temple duties. Hophni and Phinehas abused these women, perpetrating acts of defilement that shocked the community and defiled the holiness of the sanctuary. The very space consecrated to God became a place marked by oppression and violation—scandalous abuses whispered about in the marketplaces and homes of Israel. Eli's response to these grievous offenses encapsulates the tension between human frailty and divine expectation. Though he rebuked his sons for their behavior, his reprimands carried little weight, and he failed to remove them from their positions. His words, "Why do you do such things? For I hear of your evil dealings from all the people," served more as a somber warning than an effective correction. His inability or unwillingness to enforce discipline betrayed both a parental weakness and perhaps a theological misapprehension about the seriousness of the sin. This failure to act decisively allowed the decay to deepen and spread. The cultural context of this priestly corruption reveals a society at a crossroads. The period of the judges had been marked by cycles of apostasy and deliverance, a tumultuous era in which the decentralized leadership of tribal elders and charismatic judges gave way, time and again, to moral and spiritual confusion. Within this instability, the priesthood was meant to be a stabilizing institution, a living symbol of Israel's identity and covenant faithfulness. Yet here, amid the chaos, those entrusted with this vital role betrayed their calling. The result was a crisis not merely of individual sin but of societal disintegration. Religious observance became mechanical and hollow, an empty shell of true worship. The people approached the altar, not in contrition and reverence, but with frustration and alienation. The priestly abuses undermined the sacred rhythms of the community, disrupting the flow of hope and grace. The sanctuary, once a locus of God's tangible presence, teetered on the brink of desecration. The consequences of this corruption were both immediate and profound. Israel faced divine judgment not simply as the outcome of abstract doctrine, but as a living, breathing reality manifesting in national trauma. The loss of divine favor was reflected in military defeats, social unrest, and a pervasive sense of doom. The once-vibrant connection between Israel and Yahweh grew faint; the people sensed that the God of their fathers was withdrawing, a retreat mirrored in the faltering of the priesthood. Amidst this bleak landscape, the figure of Samuel emerges—a boy nurtured within these troubled surroundings but destined for a divine mission that would bring renewal and justice. His childhood, shaped by the failures and shadows of the men before him, would be the foundation for his call, a call that would confront these very evils and mark the turning point for Israel's redemption. The urgency of renewal resonates deeply through this narrative. Samuel's coming is portrayed not merely as the arrival of another leader but as a divine intervention—a necessary realignment of the people's relationship with God. His life stands in stark contrast to the moral decline of Eli's sons: humble, obedient, and sensitive to God's voice. Where corruption reigned unchecked, Samuel would embody accountability and righteousness. Scripturally and thematically, the juxtaposition between the celebration of covenant rites and the shadow of moral decay serves to highlight the tension within Israel at this pivotal moment. The images of feast and festivity, sacrifice and song, contrast with betrayal and brokenness, creating a powerful, dramatic tension. The spiritual crisis was not distant or abstract but immediate and visceral, a crisis felt in the hearts and lives of the people. This crisis also functions as a mirror for the nation's conscience, exposing how far Israel had fallen. It invites readers to consider the themes of sin and judgment, not only as historical realities but as enduring truths about the nature of human leadership, faithfulness, and divine expectation. It is within this frame that Samuel's story gains its depth and urgency. The narrative of corruption at Shiloh thus becomes a cautionary tale about the dangers of unrepentant sin in positions of power. The priesthood's failure to uphold justice invited catastrophe, illustrating that leadership detached from righteousness breeds decay and disaster. Eli's sons, through their abuses, unwittingly set the stage for their own downfall and the divine upheaval to come. In conclusion, the shadow cast by the corruption within the priesthood during Samuel's childhood reveals much about the fragile interface between human frailty and divine holiness. It is a moment frozen between past failures and future hope, between judgment and mercy. The story lays bare the cultural and religious crisis looming over Israel, making the emergence of Samuel not only plausible but necessary—a herald of a new era defined by renewal, justice, and restoration. Through this vivid contrast of decadence and divine calling, the narrative invites reflection on the cost of moral compromise and the transformational power of faithful obedience.

The Night When Heaven Called: Samuel's Divine Awakening

Silent Shadows and Sacred Voices

The temple lay cloaked in darkness, its ancient stones whispering secrets as old as time itself. Shadows danced along the walls, cast by the flickering flame of a solitary lamp resting on the altar. The soft murmur of the night was punctuated only by the distant hum of the priestly chants drifting away into memory and the occasional scurry of small creatures hidden beyond the sanctuary's edge. Within this hallowed space, the air was thick with stillness, a stillness so profound it felt nearly tangible, as if the very breath of heaven hung suspended, waiting. Samuel lay on a simple mat beside the Ark of the Covenant, his youthful body curled in tentative repose beneath the faint glow. The rough-hewn wooden beams above him absorbed and muffled the night's breath, sheltering the temple's silence like an ancient womb. Every creak, every sigh from the stones seemed magnified in the profound quietude. With eyes heavy and heart trembling between fear and hope, the boy clung to the fragile thread of wakefulness, sensing that something extraordinary stirred just beyond the reach of sight and sound. The lamp's flame wavered, casting long, quivering shadows that jittered like restless spirits upon the walls. The scent of burning oil mingled with the faint fragrance of incense lingering in the temple's recesses—a scent both comforting and unsettling, as if inviting the soul to pay unwavering attention. Samuel's breath came slow and shallow; every inhale was a silent prayer, every exhale a hesitant release of tension. His small hands clenched the coarse fabric of his cloak, knuckles pale under the amber glow. He was a boy suspended between the known and the ineffable, straddling the precarious boundary where the earthly meets the divine. It was in this crucible of profound stillness and subtle stirring of light and shadow that he first heard it: a calling not spoken in thunder or blaze, but whispered—soft yet insistent, penetrating the depths of his soul as a stone dropped into a still pool, sending ripples outward in every direction. At first, Samuel wasn't certain if he had heard anything at all. The voice, if it could be called that, was no more than a flicker at the edge of his awareness, a tremulous touch on the strings of his spirit. Moments passed, the silence folding back over itself, and the boy's heart pounded louder than the quiet voice. He blinked against the darkness, trying to understand what trembling reality was unfolding in the shadows." Samuel!" The voice came again, clearer this time, yet still gentle, like the sigh of a breeze stirring through ancient olive branches. His eyes snapped open, wide and searching. He rose on shaky knees, the rough stone beneath them cool and unmoving. Fear mixed with an exhilarating sense of wonder surged through him, a tumult he could neither name nor resist. Unsure and trembling, Samuel slipped quietly from the chamber he called home to the inner sanctum where Eli, the aged priest, slept—a guardian of the sacred mysteries, wrapped in robes the color of twilight. The boy's footsteps were so light they might have been imagined, almost afraid to disturb the hallowed serenity that enveloped the temple." Did you call me, Eli?" Samuel's voice broke the heavy silence, tentative and uncertain. The old priest stirred, eyes opening to the dimness of the night. Bewildered, his wrinkled face creased into a puzzled frown. "I did not call you, my son. Go back to your rest." But the summons lingered like an echo in Samuel's heart. With every reluctant step back to his mat, another pulse of that sacred voice pressed upon him, insistent and undeniable. He tried to sleep, yet the silence had become a living presence, alive with possibility, pregnant with mystery. Over the course of the night, the calling came again and again, a sacred refrain that pierced through the tangible darkness, an invitation to listen beyond the mere ear, to hear with the inner depths of being. Each time, Samuel sought the old priest's guidance, each time met with gentle admonition and the same denial. Eli's failing eyesight and waning strength rendered him blind to the truth unraveling quietly under the veil of night. The young boy's confusion grew; doubt crept in like a chill that gnaws endlessly at the edge of a fire's warmth. Was this a trick of the night? A mere figment of an overactive imagination, the breath of loneliness wrapped in shadows? Or was it something infinitely greater—something holy, reaching out to touch a boy's life and change the course of a nation? Here, within the temple's stone embrace, under the trembling light of the lamps, Samuel was drawn into the profound dance between silence and sound, light and shadow, fear and faith. His senses heightened, every small noise became a message, every flicker of flame a symbol, every breath a prayer. The weight of the unseen pressed upon him with both urgency and gentleness. He recognized, however faintly, that this moment was not merely about hearing a voice—it was about discerning a presence, learning the sacred art of listening when all earthly signals fall away. The divine summons was not loud or brash; it was a quiet shadow, a sacred murmur brushing against the soul in the depth of night's embrace. With the final call, a dawning clarity settled over Samuel's spirit. Eli's whispered counsel came at last: "Go, lie down again, and if you hear the voice once more, say, 'Speak, LORD, for your servant is listening.'" This was the key—a relinquishing of fear, a surrendering of the heart's grip to open fully to the mysterious will of heaven. Gathering courage like a cloak around him, Samuel obeyed. He lay down again, cloaked in the temple's darkness, the flickering lamps now seeming like distant stars winking with quiet encouragement. The silence deepened; the shadows thickened. Then the voice spoke once more. This time, there was no mistaking it. No wavering, no shadow of doubt. It was the Lord—the voice of God calling out to a servant chosen for a destiny far greater than he could comprehend." Speak, for your servant is listening." In that sacred night, beneath the watchful eyes of flickering lamps and ancient stone, Samuel's life was forever transformed. The silent shadows and sacred voices intertwined to awaken a prophet, setting the wheels of history turning toward a future weighted with promise and peril. The temple, once a place of routine and ritual, became a realm where heaven and earth touched in a moment of profound intimacy. The boy who had known only the flickering torchlight now beheld the dawn of purpose illuminated by a voice that would guide him through years of judgment, kingship, and faith. It was a night when silence itself spoke—in profound shadows and whispered calls—to reveal the sacred truth that those who listen with open hearts shall hear the voice of God, even in the darkest hours. And so began the awakening of Samuel, the servant, the prophet, the bridge between eras, chosen by a divine will that moved silently, yet with inexorable power.

Eli's Guidance: Recognizing the Call

The night had settled deep over the precincts of the Tabernacle, a quiet that seemed to breathe with the weight of expectation. For a boy like Samuel, whose life had already been touched by the extraordinary, the stillness of night was no ordinary silence. It was a threshold, carrying the subtle vibrations of something immense and unseen. Yet, the repeated awakenings of that night carried more than the disruption of rest—they carried a summons. In the dim recesses of the sanctuary, Samuel lay awake again, his senses sharpened, awakened not just by a voice but by something deeper, something that called beyond sound. As the fourth time that evening, Samuel stirred from his sleep, fully roused yet tinged with confusion, and ventured through the quiet halls toward the chamber where the aged priest Eli lay in guarded repose. The candlelight flickered, casting long shadows that danced against the ancient stones, as if the very walls held their breath in anticipation. "Here I am," Samuel whispered softly, stepping lightly into the room. Eli opened his eyes, their brightness belying the priest's many years. "I did not call you, my son," Eli said gently, though a flicker of concern crossed his face. "Return to your place and sleep once more."But the call came again, and again, and once more Samuel responded, each time returning to the side of his mentor with the same words, "Here I am."By the fourth time, Eli's gaze grew steady, his heart catching the unmistakable sign of divine visitation. The veil between heaven and earth had thinned, and a sacred mystery stood on the cusp of unfolding."Go, lie down," Eli instructed with certainty now, "and if you are called again, say this: 'Speak, Lord, for your servant is listening.'" His voice was calm but resolute, carrying the solemnity of a man who had long learned to discern the whispers of the Most High. Samuel obeyed, retreating to his rest with a new purpose. The restless stirring within his soul began to compass itself with the weight of Eli's words. When the voice came again, now unmistakably clear, Samuel's reply echoed in the stillness with quiet power: "Speak, Lord, for your servant is listening." In this moment, the boy crossed into a new realm—a sacred dialogue was initiated. Later, as dawn began to pale the sky, Eli summoned Samuel to his side. The old priest's heart was heavy yet filled with hope. "Samuel," he began, the tremor in his voice betraying a mixture of reverence and concern, "the Lord has shown forth His purpose to you tonight." Samuel's eyes were wide, the innocence of childhood still present but touched irrevocably by something ancient and profound. "What does it mean, Eli? Why has He called me so?" Eli's hands, marked by years of toil and prayer, found Samuel's small ones in a gentle grip. "The Lord speaks to those He chooses, and in calling you, He sets you upon a path not lightly taken. Obedience to His voice will be your strength, humility your guide." He paused, searching Samuel's face, seeing beyond the boy the nascent prophet. "You see, Samuel, God's call is never a summons to glory or ease. It is a partnership: one of listening and responding, of trust and faithful service, even when that service leads to loneliness or suffering." Samuel absorbed each word, feeling the weight of divine-human partnership settling deep within his soul. "I will listen, Eli. I will not turn away." Eli smiled faintly, a mixture of pride and sorrow threading through his expression. "Good, my son. Such a heart is holy ground." In the days that followed, Eli became more than a mentor—he was a spiritual guide, a voice of wisdom steering Samuel through the tempest of uncertainty that accompanies divine commissioning. Together, they wrestled with questions that had no simple answers, probing the mysteries of God's will and the burdens it places upon those who bear His message." What if I am afraid?" Samuel once confessed in the solitude of the sanctuary. Eli's reply was immediate, firm as the ancient pillars holding the Tabernacle's roof. "Then you must remember that fear need not be the master of the faithful. God does not leave His messengers alone. He is a shield in the darkness, a light when the way is lost." Through such dialogues, Samuel's understanding deepened—not only of his role but of the very nature of prophecy itself. It was not a mantle donned lightly; rather, it was a calling into the mystery of God's plan for His people, demanding obedience that transcended personal desire and human failings. Eli's teachings emphasized humility above all. "A prophet is not greater than the One who calls him," Eli reminded Samuel repeatedly. "The prophet is but a vessel—humble, willing, and open—that God's words might flow and find their place amidst the hearts of men." Samuel began to see the true dimensions of this calling: it was an intimate partnership between heaven and earth, where the human voice bore the thunder of divine judgment and hope alike. One evening, as the silver moon bathed the land, Samuel turned to Eli with a question born from the depths of his emerging faith. "Will it always be so: this dialogue between God and man? Will I hear His voice throughout my life?" Eli nodded slowly, the candlelight illuminating the lines of age and wisdom on his face. "Those who are called to be prophets carry that sacred dialogue always. But the voice may come in silence, in dreams, or sudden insight. The key is to remain faithful, to listen with an open heart, and to obey without hesitation." The theological resonance of Eli's counsel unfolded with each passing day, weaving into Samuel's very being an understanding of his role that extended far beyond the moment. It planted within him the seeds of a life lived in covenant with the divine, marked by obedience even in hardship, humility amid power, and an unwavering trust in the unseen guidance of God. Eli recognized, too that Samuel's path would be lonely. To be the voice for God meant standing between the people and their Creator, often at great personal cost. "There will be days when men will reject your words, question your authority, or seek to silence you," Eli warned. "But remember, your service is not to men, but to God alone." The weight of those words settled on Samuel's shoulders, but with it came a quiet resolve. In the tender moments that followed, Eli prayed over Samuel, entrusting the boy's future to the God who called him and beseeching protection and strength for the journey ahead. This pivotal time also transformed their relationship. No longer was Eli simply the priest guiding a boy; he became a spiritual father nurturing the birth of a prophet. Their conversations, once centered on ritual and duty, now reached into divine mysteries, exploring the complex interplay of obedience and revelation. Through those unfolding days, Samuel's innocence gave way to a burgeoning prophetic consciousness infused with deep humility. He learned that to receive God's word was a profound honor—that with it came great responsibility, and that true obedience often required surrendering one's own will to a higher purpose. Eli's guidance illuminated the truth that prophecy was less about power and more about partnership. It was a sacred trust—a covenant between human vulnerability and divine strength. As the seasons changed and Samuel grew in stature and spirit, this moment of recognition remained etched indelibly upon his heart—the night he learned to answer God, not with fear or hesitation, but with a willing and listening soul. It was the night that marked his passage from boy to prophet, from silence to speech, from waiting to active service. The lessons of obedience, humility, and divine partnership that Eli imparted found root in Samuel's life, shaping not just the boy but the future leader and judge of Israel. The divine awakening had come, but it was through Eli's sage counsel that Samuel came truly to understand what it meant to be called, and more profoundly, what it meant to listen. In the quiet aftermath, Samuel embraced his role with a clarity born of insight and faith. This was not a path he had chosen, but one he would walk with humility and courage, guided by the eternal voice that had spoken his name in the night. And so, beneath the canopy of stars that night and in the days to come, the boy who heard God's call became the prophet who would change the course of Israel's history—shaped and steady by the enduring wisdom of Eli's guidance.

Embracing Destiny

The silence of the night was profound. In that stillness, the boy named Samuel lay awake, his heart pounding with a mixture of fear and wonder. The familiar walls of the tabernacle, dimly illuminated by a flickering oil lamp, seemed both a refuge and a mystery. Beyond that sacred space, shadows stretched and shifted like restless spirits, reminding him of the unseen realities that hovered at the edge of human perception. It was in this suspended moment between darkness and dawn that Samuel's soul began to stir, awakening to an invisible call that would forever alter the course of his life. For a long time, confusion had clouded his mind. The voice—the divine utterance—had come not once, but three times, each time pulling him further from the security of boyhood innocence and toward a destiny unknown. With every call, a new weight settled upon him, a summons that unsettled his very being. Yet, fear and uncertainty had tangled with curiosity and faith, leaving Samuel hesitant to step forward. This night, however, marked a turning point. The final hesitation began to unravel. As the first grey light of dawn filtered through the curtained entrance, Samuel felt the darkness within him begin to dissipate, chased away by rays of understanding that glimmered like stars surrendering to morning. In the quiet that followed, a delicate clarity emerged — a whisper of purpose that transcended doubt. He realized that the voice which had roused him from sleep was not a call to mere service, but an invitation to partnership with the eternal, a communion that would shape the destiny of a nation. In this moment of profound awakening, the boy's apprehension gave way to resolve. The apprehensive edges of his youth softened into the contours of determined faith. It was not merely the acceptance of a task, but the embracing of an identity—prophet, judge, and servant of the Most High. The weight that once felt overwhelming transformed into a mantle of sacred responsibility, a burden borne with humility yet fierce courage. Samuel understood that God did not call the perfect or the ready, but the willing. The imagery of this transformation was etched deeply into the quiet hours: light breaking through a canopy of shadows, piercing the gloom with rays that revealed the path ahead. The tabernacle, once a place of shelter, became a gateway to the divine. Samuel's heart, once shrouded in uncertainty, opened like a flower facing the dawn. This awakening was not just a moment of revelation but a beginning—a spiritual rebirth that ignited a fire within him, one that would burn through trials and triumphs alike. To step into God's calling is to stand at the precipice of the unknown, where human frailty confronts divine power. Samuel's story captures this paradox—the tension between fear and faith, between doubt and obedience. His acceptance was not a dramatic proclamation but a quiet yielding, an inner surrender that acknowledged both his limitations and the boundless strength of the One who called him. In embracing this destiny, Samuel exemplified a truth that resonates through the ages: that divine purpose often unfolds in the humility of trust rather than the certainty of control. Yet, even as this new dawn illuminated Samuel's path, shadows lingered on the horizon. The journey ahead would be fraught with challenges—resistance from worldly powers, moments of loneliness, and the heavy burden of leading a fractured people. The close of night's mystery did not promise ease; it heralded conflict, growth, and transformation. This acceptance was merely the threshold. Samuel's faith would be tested, and his leadership forged in the crucible of experience. The narrative breathes with an undercurrent of suspense, foreshadowing the complex tapestry of events yet to unfold. The boy who heard God's voice in the dark would soon anoint Israel's first king, confront a monarch's pride, and anoint a shepherd boy whose heart beat in rhythm with God's own. Each step Samuel would take was mapped by divine purpose yet challenged by human frailty. His life embodies the profound tension of being God's instrument in a fallen world—a reminder that the path of calling is both sacred and perilous. As dawn gave way to morning, Samuel rose, his spirit renewed and his heart aligned with the will of Heaven. What had once been a night of uncertainty had become a foundation stone of faith. The journey from the shadows into the light had begun—not as a sudden leap, but a steady ascent marked by trust, obedience, and the quiet courage of a servant. This was Samuel's divine awakening, a moment where heaven's voice met earth's soul, and a boy stepped forward to embrace a destiny that would echo through

generations. In this silence before the day's stirring, the world itself seemed to hold its breath, as if awaiting the unfolding story of a prophet who would walk through history's shadows into the brilliance of God's purpose. Samuel's destiny was no longer a distant dream but a living reality—one that would demand everything he was and all he could become. It was the sacred embrace of a calling that neither sheltered him from hardship nor guaranteed earthly triumph, but promised the unyielding presence of God in every step. Thus, the night when heaven called did not end in silence but began in song—the song of a life surrendered, of faith ignited, and of destiny embraced, weaving the first threads in the untold chronicles of a prophet whose journey through the ages would inspire the hearts of seekers yet to come.

A Judge Rises: Steering Israel Through Turmoil

Council Chambers and Tribal Fires

The sun was dipping low over the rugged hills of Israel, casting long shadows across the uneven terrain where tribes congregated, their faces etched with a mix of hope and worry. The air was thick with the unmistakable scent of woodsmoke mingled with the musky aroma of armor and worn leather. In these hours, the boundaries of ancient tribal territories seemed to blur, as the people's fate hung in the balance—a nation trembling at the crossroads between chaos and order. At the heart of this restless era stood Samuel, the judge appointed not only by divine command but also by widespread clamors for leadership amid relentless upheaval. His story was inseparable from the political and spiritual turbulence that rocked Israel, a landscape defined by fractious councils, simmering rivalries, and the looming threat of war. To understand how Samuel guided this fragile cast of tribes through such stormy seas, one must first step beyond the sacred scrolls into the council chambers and tribal fires, where voices rose sharp and strong, and destinies were forged in the heat of debate. The council chamber, more a vast enclosure beneath a canopy of ancient olive and carob trees than a formal hall, was the pulsing heart of Israel's fragile unity. Here, the chieftains, elders, and warriors of the twelve tribes gathered—each bearing the weight of his people's hopes and histories. The stones beneath their feet, scattered and weathered, told stories of countless assemblies, of verdicts reached and promises sworn. The open sky overhead was sometimes their only roof, the chilly air filled with murmurs, sharp arguments, and the low hum of sacred song. Samuel's presence was a lodestone—steady and commanding, yet touched with a humility born of his divine calling. He did not preside with the pomp of a monarch, for Israel sought no king yet.

Instead, his authority lay in wisdom, conviction, and an unwavering commitment to the covenant between God and His people. The elders and chieftains debated fiercely in his presence, their voices rising and falling like waves, each tribe guarding its traditions and grievances as fiercely as its grazing lands." It is not enough to simply gather and lament," one tribal leader snapped during a particularly heated dispute. His cloak, heavy with the threads of his lineage, rustled as he leaned forward. "Our resolve must be sharpened like the spear—our enemies are at our gates, and fear will only bring ruin." Another, younger and from the rugged hills of Ephraim, countered, "And if we rush headlong, what becomes of the children, and the fields we must defend? Strength is in wisdom as much as steel." His eyes betrayed sleepless nights and the weight of too much loss. Across the circle, murmurs rose. The tribes had long been divided—by geography, by kinship, and by the age-old suspicion sewn in the memories of past betrayals. The scars from the days when the Philistines rode unchecked across their land were still fresh in many minds. Samuel listened, weighing every word, every pause, his mind ever turning to the covenant and the words of the Lord that had called him from the sanctuary at Shiloh. The clatter that often interrupted these deliberations was no less telling of the times—clattering armor being fitted and adjusted, the metallic ring of a sword sliding back into its sheath, the steady thud of leather shields against shields in preparation. Warriors flanked the council, faces glistening with sweat, muscles taut beneath worn tunics, standing ready to heed their leaders' call to battle if peace could not be brokered. Their presence was both a reassurance and a stark reminder of the precariousness of the moment. Amidst the debates, Samuel's voice would rise—not loud, but edged with the unmistakable authority of one who walks with the divine. "We must remember," he said once, "that we are not united by the strength of our arms alone but by the faith we bear in the Lord's promises. Our battles are not only fought against men but with the spirit, and it is that spirit which must lead." By the light of flickering torches, as the day waned and night crept over the camp, discussions often shifted from harsh political exchange to more solemn spiritual counsel. The tribes, though wary of one another, were also fiercely bound by a common faith. Their covenant with the God of Abraham and Moses was the invisible thread holding them together, however frayed. Around blazing fires outside the council circle, the elders would whisper prayers and psalms, the smoke entwining with the night air as if to carry their pleas heavenward. This spiritual undercurrent permeated every decision, every diplomatic maneuver. Even as Samuel prepared to send emissaries to the outlying tribes, urging them to rally for defense against a new Philistine incursion, he moved with the awareness that Israel's salvation depended not solely on the strength of swords but on obedience and repentance. The campfires themselves were alive with stories and songs—tales of past victories and humiliations, of patriarchs wandering the desert, of divine interventions and sacred laws. These tales were often recited by aged bards or whispered by mothers to their children, weaving identity and resolve into the very air. The flickering flames cast dancing shadows on weathered faces, a reminder of the weight of history carried by each generation. In these moments, it was clear that while politics played out in heated words and council chambers, the true engine of Israel's resilience was the faith that bound its people. Samuel, as the divine judge, was the bridge between temporal governance and spiritual stewardship, tasked with uniting a fractious nation under covenantal law. Yet the divisions ran deep. Tribe pressed against tribe, old wounds refused to heal easily. The hill country of Benjamin and the plains of Judah often found themselves at odds over land and influence, while the northern tribes eyed the south with suspicion. The centuries-old rivalries and grudges were as potent as the Philistine spear or the Ammonite arrow. One evening, after a particularly fractious session of the council, Samuel walked alone among the encampments. The distant laughter of children echoed across the valley, mingling with the muted conversations of soldiers preparing for the coming days. The air was cool, the stars beginning to prick the sky like divine watchfires. It was in this solitude that Samuel wrestled with the enormous burden placed upon him. To be a judge in Israel was no mere title; it was a task soaked in sacrifice and peril. The tribes looked to him to hold the fractious factions together, to steer them true through the trials of war and political intrigue, and to maintain the delicate balance between human authority and divine will. The sound of a distant drum called him back to the council chamber for a midnight meeting—a summons that reminded him that even in the quiet of night, the work was never done. As he returned, the glow of fires and the murmurs of soldiers in their tents reminded him of the immense responsibility resting on his shoulders. The preparations for war were as somber as the discussions that preceded them. From dawn till dusk, he oversaw the marshalling of troops, the sharpening of blades, the steady influx of supplies and intelligence. His judgments on disputes, his pronouncements of divine will, were interspersed with moments of quiet counsel and encouragement to those who feared the coming storm. The smoky camps where warriors gathered carried a raw vitality—men and women who had known hardship and loss, united by a shared purpose though often divided by ancestral lines. The flicker of campfires illuminated faces calloused by toil but softened in prayer. The smell of warming meat and damp earth, combined with the metallic tang of weapons; these sensory details etched a vivid image of a nation poised on the edge of transformation. But Samuel's leadership never devolved into mere force or strategy. He reminded the tribes—and indeed himself—that the sword was but a tool, and that Israel's true strength lay in holiness, unity, and humility before God. Between the clamor of heated council debates and the tense silence of nights spent by the flickering tribal fires, his voice remained a beacon calling Israel to a higher purpose. Thus, in council chambers filled with clattering armor and sharp exchanges, and beside tribal fires glowing through restless nights, Samuel rose—not as a king crowned in splendor, but as a shepherd of a people clinging to faith amid turmoil. It was in these raw moments— where political acumen met spiritual devotion—that the fabric of Israel's destiny began to be rewoven, with Samuel at its center, steering them through chaos toward a new dawn.

Samuel's Judgements and Divinely Guided Decisions

Samuel's role as judge and leader in Israel was far more than a position of authority; it was a divine commission that demanded wisdom, discernment, and an unwavering commitment to justice. In an age marred by moral decay, political instability, and spiritual confusion, Samuel's judgements served as both a spiritual anchor and a practical guidepost for a nation in desperate need of direction. His decisions bore the weight not merely of legal outcomes but of spiritual consequences, reflecting an intricate interplay between divine revelation and tangible governance. Through an examination of key judicial episodes and the nuanced processes behind Samuel's rulings, we see a portrait of a leader who embodied justice as a sacred trust, exemplifying the profound responsibilities inherent in shepherding a people under God's watchful eye. At the heart of Samuel's judicial role was the recognition that true leadership could never be divorced from divine guidance. Unlike the secular judges who came before him, Samuel's authority was irrevocably tied to his prophetic vocation. His decisions were not grounded solely in human reasoning but were infused with the insight and mandate given by the Lord. This convergence of roles — prophet, judge, and priest — endowed Samuel's governance with a unique legitimacy and seriousness, one that underscored the inseparable nature of spiritual and civil leadership in ancient Israel. One of the most illuminating examples of Samuel's judgements can be seen in his work resolving disputes among the people and confronting crises that threatened national cohesion. The biblical record recounts how the Israelites would come to Samuel at Ramah to seek justice, bringing their grievances and conflicts before him for resolution. The accounts, though sparse in detail, reveal a pattern of deliberation marked by fairness, impartiality, and a deep reverence for God's law. Samuel was not merely an administrator handing down verdicts; he was a mediator tasked with discerning the divine will in complex and often contentious situations. In each case, Samuel's decisions were characterized by an unwavering commitment to equity.

The biblical narrative, in depicting Samuel's impartiality, highlights the danger of favoritism and partiality that had plagued Israel's previous leaders and judges. For Samuel, the law was a sacred covenant, and each judgement was an opportunity to uphold God's justice rather than human preference. This posture reflected a profound theological truth: that justice is not merely a human aspiration but a divine imperative, an expression of God's own nature. Samuel's role as judge thus becomes a reflection of God's character, stewarding his people in righteousness and truth. Accounts from the text illustrate moments when Samuel did more than judge — he prayed fervently for guidance, consulting the Lord before issuing decisions. This emphasis on prayer and revelation distinguishes Samuel's leadership profoundly. It is one thing to be a wise judge; it is another to be a conduit of divine will, whose decisions are shaped by an ongoing dialogue with God. This ongoing consultation with the divine highlights an essential principle: earthly authority must remain subordinate to heavenly authority. Samuel's example illustrates that human wisdom alone is insufficient for righteous governance; it must be tempered and informed by spiritual insight. A particularly revealing judicial episode involves the resolution of disputes arising from military confrontations or internal strife, in which Samuel's role shifted from adjudicator to peacemaker. The stabilization of the tribes following periods of chaos required more than legal pronouncements; it called for restoration, reconciliation, and renewed commitment to God's covenant. Samuel's decisions often bore this restorative character, actively seeking to reorient Israel's fractured society toward unity and obedience to divine statutes. By doing so, Samuel underscored justice as an instrument of healing rather than merely punishment or retribution. Moreover, the way Samuel handled the delicate matter of leadership succession sheds light on his judicial philosophy. When the time came to anoint a king, Samuel faced an unprecedented challenge: reconciling Israel's growing demand for monarchy with God's sovereignty and the risks inherent in human rulership. His decision to anoint Saul — and later David — was guided by careful discernment and prophetic insight, rather than political expediency or popular opinion. This moment demonstrates Samuel's role not only as judge but as kingmaker, a mediator of God's will at a critical historical juncture. His judgements in these matters were not merely administrative but prophetic acts that shaped Israel's destiny. Throughout Samuel's tenure as judge, there is also a striking integration of ritual and law. His judicial decisions often took place within liturgical or sacrificial contexts, reinforcing the link between law and worship. This ritual dimension of judgement underscored the theological claim that justice is ultimately enacted in the presence of God, the true judge of all. Such a setting elevated the process of judgement beyond mere human arbitration, imbuing it with solemnity and divine witness. It serves as a powerful reminder that justice in Israel was not a secular procedure but a sacred covenantal act that bound both rulers and the ruled. The personal burdens that accompanied such a sacred charge are echoed in the biblical narrative as well. Samuel, while resolute and wise, is shown bearing the weight of responsibility heavily, aware that his judgements carried eternal significance. This portrayal humanizes the prophet, reminding readers that leadership, especially that which seeks to mirror God's justice, comes at a profound personal cost. The loneliness, the moral dilemmas, and the constant vigilance required are part and parcel of the prophetic vocation. Samuel's endurance through these challenges exemplifies a steadfast faith in God's guidance even in the face of daunting difficulties and opposition. From a theological perspective, Samuel's judgements embody the principle that divine justice is inseparable from mercy and covenant fidelity. His rulings consistently reflected an attempt to balance strict adherence to God's law with compassion for the people's covenantal journey. Rather than wielding power in a harsh, authoritarian manner, Samuel's leadership emphasized corrective justice — one that aimed to restore the people's relationship with God and each other. In this sense, his judgements were formative, shaping the moral and spiritual character of Israel rather than merely settling disputes. This theological nuance is crucial for understanding the broader significance of Samuel's role. His judgements do not exist in isolation but are part of a larger divine economy in which God's covenant with Israel is continually renewed and tested. Samuel's office was that of a covenant mediator: every ruling he pronounced had to preserve the sacred obligations binding Israel to Yahweh. Failure in judgement was therefore more than a legal misstep; it risked jeopardizing the very covenantal relationship that defined Israel's identity. This framework imbues every judicial decision with cosmic importance, reminding leaders and laity alike that justice serves the ultimate purpose of sustaining God's kingdom on earth. One of the more subtle aspects of Samuel's judicial leadership was his ability to navigate the tension between divine sovereignty and human agency. While his decisions were grounded in the revelation of God's will, they also required practical wisdom, political savvy, and an understanding of human nature. Samuel's governance was therefore as much about navigating human complexities as it was about declaring divine mandates. This dynamic highlights a critical leadership lesson: true authority must balance transcendent principles with pragmatic realities, ensuring that justice is both righteous and effective. Samuel's judgements also demonstrate a profound trust in God's timing and purposes. Unlike leaders who might rush decisions for political gain or expediency, Samuel displayed patience and steadfastness, allowing space for divine intervention and revelation. His willingness to await God's direction before acting underscores a deep spiritual maturity and humility, qualities essential for anyone who seeks to wield authority under divine mandate. This patient posture serves as a counterpoint to the often hurried and unilateral decision-making seen in secular contexts, modeling a leadership grounded in faith and reflection. Historically, Samuel's judicial role marked a vital transition for Israel. The period of the judges was characterized by decentralized, tribe-based leadership prone to cycles of violence and disunity. Samuel's emergence heralded a more centralized and stable form of governance under God's guidance, setting the stage for the monarchy. His judgements functioned not only as mechanisms for resolving individual disputes but as instruments for nation-building and spiritual restoration. By embodying both prophet and judge, Samuel bridged past traditions and future hopes, crafting a leadership legacy that would influence Israelite polity for generations. The biblical text hints at the struggles Samuel faced in maintaining this balance of spiritual insight, justice, and political leadership. The demands of the office meant contending with entrenched interests, rival factions, and the people's often fickle loyalty. Yet Samuel's steadfastness in holding firm to divine principles exemplifies the ideal of the righteous leader — one who prioritizes faithfulness over popularity and truth over convenience. His example challenges contemporary readers to consider the moral weight that leaders bear and the profound courage required to lead in fidelity to divine justice. In reflecting on Samuel's judgements, it becomes evident that his leadership was much more than a series of legal decisions. It was a continuous act of worship and obedience, a manifestation of his calling to serve as God's emissary among the people. Each ruling carried layers of meaning — legal, moral, spiritual — that together formed a coherent vision of a just and holy community. Samuel's legacy, therefore, is not simply that of a successful judge but of a sacred steward of God's justice, whose decisions helped to establish a lasting foundation for Israel's political and spiritual life. The intricate fusion of divine instruction and pragmatic governance in Samuel's work provides timeless insights into the nature of leadership. His judgements remind us that true authority is exercised in humility before God, with a commitment to fairness, mercy, and truth. They demonstrate that governing a people under God's covenant is not merely an administrative task but a sacred trust that calls for continual prayer, reflection, and courage. In a world often marked by moral ambiguity and political turmoil, Samuel's example shines as a beacon — an enduring testimony to leadership that seeks first the justice of the Most High. As we continue to explore the convoluted and challenging period in which Samuel lived, his judgements stand as milestones of divine fidelity amid human uncertainty. They call leaders and citizens alike to remember that governance, when rightly understood, serves a higher purpose: to reflect God's justice on earth and to foster a community grounded in covenant love. Samuel's life and decisions thus become a model not only for ancient

Israel but for all who seek to lead with righteousness, wisdom, and faith.

Bringing Unity Amidst Discord

The land of Israel during Samuel's era was a tapestry of fractured tribes, each with its own loyalties, fears, and grievances. Amid this landscape of fragmented people, besieged not only by external foes but also internal discord, the figure of Samuel emerged as a beacon of unity. His mission was daunting: to forge a cohesive nation where division threatened to unravel the very fabric of Israelite identity. This subchapter unfolds the intricate journey Samuel undertook to bring the disparate tribes into a single fold, revealing how battlefield valor, sagacious diplomacy, and prophetic authority intertwined to create a fragile but steadfast unity. The immediate context was grim. The Philistines, Israel's persistent adversaries, were growing bolder, pressing into Israelite territory with increasing frequency and ruthlessness. The tribes, while sharing a common ancestry and faith, were often more concerned with local survival and rivalries than with a larger national identity. The memories of past victories were overshadowed by the fear of annihilation, and suspicion among the tribes hampered any collective response. In this crucible, Samuel's leadership was called forth — not merely as a military commander, but as a spiritual guide and unifying force. Samuel's first assurances to the people were not of grand promises but of a humble commitment to lead by example in faithfulness and courage. He understood that unity could not be decreed; it had to be cultivated through shared purpose and trust. His prophetic voice became an instrument to remind Israel of their covenant with God—a calling to transcend tribal divisions for a higher purpose. One of the first decisive moments in Samuel's pursuit of unity came when he appealed to the Israelites to assemble at Mizpah, a place of symbolic significance to many tribes. The gathering was a monumental undertaking. News had to travel through hostile terrain; wary chieftains had to be persuaded; the people had to overcome their fear and skepticism. Samuel's presence was magnetic, underscored by the weight of his reputation as a man chosen by God. Yet it was his sincerity and the urgency of his call that stirred the hearts of the assembly. At Mizpah, the assembly was more than a military encampment; it was a convergence of hopes and doubts. Samuel's prophetic exhortations echoed over the gathered masses, reminding them of their shared heritage—their deliverance from Egypt, the wilderness wanderings, and at last their settlement in the promised land. He spoke of the covenantal relationship with Yahweh, urging the tribes to forsake the idols and practices that fragmented their worship and to recommit themselves entirely to the one God of Israel. His words were not just religious rhetoric; they were a call to realign the people's identity around a divine mission. The urgency in Samuel's voice was palpable because the threat was immediate. At that moment, the Philistine army was advancing to exploit the disarray within Israel. Samuel organized the Israelites into a united fighting force. His military planning demonstrated both strategic acumen and a deep understanding of each tribe's strengths and weaknesses. He recognized that these tribes, despite their differences, wielded varying skills—some famed for their infantry, others for archery or knowledge of local terrain. Samuel's battlefield strategy was unconventional but effective: rather than attempting to impose a rigid command structure reminiscent of traditional armies, he delegated leadership to local chieftains while fostering an overarching unity through common ritual and purpose. Before descending into battle, he led the people in the offering of sacrifices and prayed fervently for divine intervention. These spiritual acts unified the soldiers with a sense of sacred mission, transforming the battle from a mere clash of arms into a fight for the nation's soul. The battle that ensued beneath the hot sun near Mizpah was harrowing. The emotional landscape was as tumultuous as the physical. The Israelite tribes fought shoulder to shoulder, their earlier suspicions momentarily set aside by the immediacy of survival. The terror of the Philistine war machine was intimidating, but the Israelites drew strength from the collective hope that God was with them. Samuel moved among the ranks, bolstering morale, offering prayers, and sharing the burden of fear and hope. His presence was a living testament to the possibility of unity and victory. When the dust settled and the Philistines retreated, the victory was not only military but symbolic. It was proof that the Israelite tribes could stand together, a hard-won validation of Samuel's vision. Yet the prophet knew better than to rest on battlefield laurels; true unity required more enduring ties than a fleeting alliance in war. In the aftermath, Samuel initiated a series of diplomatic missions to solidify relationships among the tribes. His approach was nuanced. He understood that marriage alliances, trade arrangements, and shared religious festivals could foster lasting bonds beyond the battlefield. He sent envoys to the tribes, engaging with their elders and leaders, listening to their grievances, and mediating disputes that lurked beneath the surface. Samuel's diplomatic efforts were deeply influenced by his prophetic conviction that the unity of Israel was a divine mandate. He invoked the stories of patriarchs, judges, and earlier prophets to remind the tribes of a shared destiny that transcended petty conflicts. His charisma and spiritual authority softened hardened hearts and built bridges where suspicion had festered. Not all tribes were immediately receptive. Some chieftains feared losing autonomy or felt slighted by historical wounds. Others were wary of Samuel's growing influence, suspecting that centralized power might eclipse their local authority. These tensions required delicate navigation. Samuel combined firmness with humility—he would not force unity, but neither would he yield when the stakes were too high. Among these internal challenges, Samuel's prophetic role took on a heightened significance. His declarations often cut through political machinations with unflinching honesty. When the tribes drifted back into idolatry or internal quarrels, Samuel confronted them boldly, sometimes with sharp rebuke, other times with impassioned appeals. His prophetic voice was a moral compass, urging the people to see beyond transient conflicts and to embrace the higher covenantal ideal. This spiritual dynamic offered the people a shared narrative and purpose. Israel was not simply a loose alliance of tribes but the chosen people called to live under God's law. This vision instilled a sense of common identity and destiny uncommon in tribal nations of the time. It created a psychological and emotional unity difficult to break, even in the face of ongoing external threats. Samuel also recognized the power of ritual and worship to bind the nation. Under his guidance, religious festivals became occasions for the tribes to come together, celebrate shared heritage, and renew their commitment to God and each other. These ceremonies heightened communal solidarity and reminded the Israelites of the sacred covenant anchoring their national identity. Within the emotional undercurrents of this turbulent time, hope mingled with anxiety. Many Israelites had lived through cycles of triumph and defeat, prosperity and famine, faithfulness and apostasy. The scars of these oscillations lingered in the collective memory. Samuel was acutely aware of this frailty and worked tirelessly to nurture perseverance and faith. At the heart of Samuel's efforts was a profound understanding that unity was more than a strategic advantage—it was an expression of covenantal obedience and spiritual vitality. The people's political cohesion mirrored their relationship with God. Thus, every negotiation, every exhortation, every battle plan was infused with this sacred dimension. Yet, despite these successes, Samuel faced the sobering reality of human imperfection. Rivalries remained, and mistrust sometimes reemerged, threatening to undo fragile alliances. Samuel's leadership was tested as he sought to maintain balance between authority and freedom, between prophetic insistence and respect for tribal autonomy. His experience forged a leadership style that was simultaneously firm and compassionate. The story of Samuel uniting Israel amidst discord is therefore a story of human complexity—the meeting of divine vision and human frailty. It is a testament to the power of faith-inspired leadership to shape history amid uncertainty and fear. In this crucible of nation-building, Samuel modeled the qualities Israel desperately needed: unwavering faith, courage under pressure, wisdom in counsel, and a heart devoted to justice and peace. His journey was not a single grand gesture but a steady march of incremental acts—prayers, speeches, battles, negotiations—that together wove a tapestry of unity. The emotional landscape within the tribes during this time was turbulent but transformative. Fear of the Philistines compelled warriors into battle, yet hope in Samuel's vision kindled determination beyond mere self-preservation. Ancient rivalries softened as shared meals were broken and offerings lifted. Skepticism gave way to tentative trust, fragile yet real. If the tribes could hold fast to this unity, the future of Israel brightened. Samuel knew that the foundational work he labored over was a gift not only to his generation but also to all who would inherit the land. His efforts planted the seeds for a kingdom that would stand beyond the era of judges—a kingdom with a king, but one rooted in covenant and conscience. Thus, the story of bringing unity amidst discord is more than a chapter in history; it is a timeless lesson. It is a reminder that unity requires courage to face both external threats and internal shadows, that leadership calls for a harmonizing of strength and humility, and that faith in a higher purpose can transform discord into community. Samuel's legacy is the legacy of a people called to be one—not by force or coercion, but through a shared vision inspired by the divine and nurtured by human hands. His story challenges us to consider how unity might be found today, amidst our own fears and divisions, if we too can summon hope, listen deeply, and act with the courage of

conviction. In the years that followed Samuel's efforts at Mizpah, the unity he forged endured, though tested repeatedly. His influence remained a rallying point as Israel faced new challenges, and his example became a touchstone for future leaders. The prophet's journey in knitting Israel together was an essential chapter in the unfolding story of a nation destined for greatness, anchored in faith and bound by a collective spirit. Through strategies on the battlefield, dialogues in tribal councils, and the fervor of prophetic proclamation, Samuel steered Israel through one of its most perilous eras. He transformed discord into a united front, instilling in the people a shared identity and destiny. This was the dawn of a new chapter—not only for Israel but for the unfolding narrative of hope, resilience, and divine promise that would resonate through the ages.

The Spiritual Revival

As the shadow of foreign oppression lingered and internal discord threatened to unravel the fabric of Israelite society, Samuel recognized that the path to national restoration could not be secured through military might or political maneuvering alone. The heart of Israel's renewal must begin with a revival of faith — a profound turning back to Yahweh, their covenant God, whose presence and favor had once distinguished Israel among the nations. Thus, toward the close of his tenure as judge and prophet, Samuel embarked upon a campaign to rekindle the spiritual flame that had waned under years of neglect and idolatry. The revival was no mere ritualistic gesture or superficial display of piety. It was an intentional, communal act of repentance and recommitment designed to cleanse the people's souls and renew their covenantal relationship with Yahweh. Samuel's efforts were rooted deeply in the ancient traditions of Israel, drawing upon the rhythms of public worship, the power of symbolic acts, and the sheer force of heartfelt prayer. From the bustling marketplaces of towns to the quiet courtyards of households, the call to return to God echoed relentlessly, inviting every Israelite to enter into a collective journey of spiritual restoration. Central to this revival were the public ceremonies Samuel orchestrated, gatherings that drew tens of thousands from all twelve tribes. These events transcended mere formality; they were dynamic encounters between the divine and the people, moments charged with solemnity and joy, fear and hope. Under vast open skies, in places hallowed by tradition, Israel came together to remember their past, confess their transgressions, and pledge renewed allegiance to Yahweh. The land itself seemed to respond, as the natural elements reflected and magnified the dramatic intensity of these occasions. The introductory rites of the ceremonies often involved water as a motif of purification. Wells and streams near the assembly sites were carefully chosen, their flowing waters symbolizing the cleansing of sin and the washing away of guilt. Participants dipped their hands and faces into the cool streams, a tangible sign of personal humility and a yearning to be made clean. In some instances, vessels filled with water were poured upon sacrificial altars, amplifying the metaphor of spiritual cleansing. The water did not merely serve as a physical agent; it flowed as a living symbol of the renewing power of Yahweh's grace. Conversely, fire played a complementary role, igniting the hearts of the faithful and manifesting the purifying presence of God. Bonfires blazed as twilight deepened, their flames licking the dusky air as prophetic prayers soared skyward. Torches were carried in solemn processions, their flickering light illuminating faces uplifted in hope and repentance. The fire was a reminder of Yahweh's holy presence, akin to the burning bush that once spoke to Moses or the pillar of fire that guided Israel through the wilderness. It was both a test of faith and a beacon of divine favor, reinforcing that God was watching and ready to act among His people. The wind, subtle yet powerful, threaded through these gatherings, its invisible breath stirring the crowds and symbolizing the Spirit of God moving among them. When prayers reached their crescendo, a sudden breeze might ripple through the assembly, whispering a promise of change and fresh beginnings. Just as the Spirit had inspired the judges before Samuel's time, bringing courage and wisdom, so now it was understood to sanctify this new chapter in Israel's history. The wind served as a divine messenger, carrying the petitions and songs of the people upward, animating the communal desire for transformation. Among these grand public events were the moments of intimate communal religious life that Samuel fostered, emphasizing that revival was not confined to formal gatherings but lived out daily in homes and neighborhoods. Families were encouraged to speak openly of their faith, to teach the statutes of Yahweh to their children, and to pray together regularly. The ancient practice of the mezuzah — affixing scripture to doorposts — experienced renewed vigor, as households sought visible reminders of God's covenant. Meals incorporated prayers of thanksgiving, and elders passed down stories of God's mighty acts, knitting faith more deeply into the fabric of everyday existence. Samuel was deeply aware that spiritual renewal required corresponding social reform. The revival was not to remain a mere affair of ritual but had to reach the ethical and political spheres, purging injustices that had proliferated during the years of moral decay. Samuel's calls for repentance included a demand for fairness in the courts, protection for widows and orphans, and the restoration of honesty among leaders. The prophetic voice grew strong against oppression, challenging the powerful who exploited the vulnerable. These reforms gradually restored trust in governance, signifying that political renewal was impossible without the underpinning of spiritual integrity. One of the most stirring moments of the revival was the public reaffirmation of the covenant at Mizpah, where the people gathered under Samuel's leadership in a solemn assembly. Here, Samuel summoned the tribes to stand as one, to hear the demands of the law read aloud, and to pledge anew their allegiance to Yahweh alone. The event was marked by tears and laughter, weeping and chanting, as Israel acknowledged past failings but also voiced hope for future faithfulness. When Samuel offered sacrifices, prayers, and prophetic exhortations, the presence of the Lord was palpably felt, settling over the people like a protective mantle. At the heart of Samuel's revival was the reinvigoration of prayer as a vital spiritual discipline, both corporate and personal. Samuel himself personified this practice, rising early and staying late in communion with God, modeling dependence not on human strength but on divine guidance. He often prayed aloud, with the voice of a judge bearing the weight of the nation's future. His prayers combined petition and praise, confession and intercession, reflecting a mature and nuanced spiritual life. This fervency inspired others — leaders, elders, and common folk alike — to adopt a similar posture of humble seeking before God. The revival also featured an emphasis on sacred music and poetry. Psalms and hymns echoed through the temple courts, voiced by men and women moved to lift their spirits and fortify their resolve. The arts became an avenue of worship and emotional expression, bridging the gap between doctrine and lived experience. These songs recounted the stories of deliverance — from Egypt to the wilderness wanderings — reminding Israel of God's faithfulness and power. Through this creative expression, the people found renewed identity and solidarity, their souls swelling with hope. Moreover, Samuel's revival addressed the role of the priesthood and the temple as central to Israel's spiritual life. He worked closely with Eli's descendants to revitalize temple worship, ensuring that the sacrifices were conducted with reverence and adherence to law. Removing corrupt practices where they had taken hold, Samuel reasserted the holiness of the tabernacle, making it a beacon of purity amidst a nation thirsting for restoration. The priests were called not only to perform rituals but to serve as teachers and guardians of the covenant, guiding the people back to the heart of Yahweh's commandments. Throughout this period, the tangible expressions of the revival — fire, water, and wind — became woven into the collective memory and spiritual language of Israel. Fire was invoked in tales of judgment and light; water remained the emblem of cleansing and rebirth; wind symbolized God's mysterious and renewing presence. These motifs transcended the immediate context of the revival, entering into liturgical practice and shaping Israel's theological imagination for generations to come. Yet, Samuel's revival was not without its tensions. The intense focus on Yahweh inevitably challenged entrenched power structures and pagan influences that had grown complacent over years of chaotic leadership. At times, resistance surfaced in subtle opposition or outright rebellion, reminding everyone that genuine renewal demanded perseverance and sacrifice. Samuel's patient yet firm leadership ensured that the revival was steady rather than fleeting, an enduring movement rather than a passing emotion. In sum, Samuel's spiritual revival was a profound convergence of public spectacle and personal transformation, of tradition renewed and innovation embraced. It was an effort to heal a fractured nation by restoring not only religious observance but also the covenantal heart that bound Israel to Yahweh. Through ceremonies rich with symbolism, fervent prayers stirred by divine inspiration, and reforms that extended into social justice, Samuel fashioned a model of revival that intertwined the sacred and the civic. The legacy of this revival endured beyond Samuel's lifetime, planting seeds of faith that would sustain Israel through the turbulent years of monarchy and exile that lay ahead. More than a historical moment, it became a template for prophetic leadership — a demonstration that true power lies in drawing people back to God, that political stability is inseparable from spiritual fidelity, and that renewal, when anchored in divine covenant, can kindle hope even in the darkest of times. As the chapter closes, one sees Samuel not just as a judge or prophet but as a shepherd of souls, guiding Israel from the desolation of estrangement back into the warmth of Yahweh's embrace. His revival was not merely a series of events, but a transformative movement, a breath of sacred wind sweeping across a parched land, igniting flames of devotion, and washing hearts anew with living water — a living testament to the power of faith revived.

Gary E. Risenhoover

Anointing the First King: Saul's Crown and Collapse

Saul's Rise: From Humble Beginnings to Crowned Glory

In the vast, rolling hills of the hill country of Benjamin, under the expansive azure sky, an ordinary man tended to his father's donkeys, unaware that his life was about to be shattered and recast by the hand of destiny. Saul, the son of Kish, was not a figure of grandeur or status; he was a man rooted in the soil of his homeland, simple in appearance yet tall and striking—a man who carried within him the latent spark of leadership that was waiting to be kindled. His rise from this quiet, pastoral life to the throne of Israel was as sudden as it was dramatic, a journey that would not only transform him but also signal the beginning of a new era in Israel's history. Israel, at this pivotal moment, stood at a crossroads. The period of the judges was drawing to a close, a time marked by tribal disunity, intermittent oppression, and sporadic deliverances. The land had known chaos, with peoples rising and falling, the tribes often at odds, lacking a central authority to unify them or lead them confidently against the threats poised by surrounding nations. The dream of a monarchy— steadfast, centralized, and mighty—had long simmered beneath the surface of Israelite consciousness, a desire whispered from one generation to the next as a hope for stability and strength. Into this atmosphere of anticipation and uncertainty came Samuel, the prophet and judge, resolved to anoint the people's first king. Saul's elevation to kingship is full of poignant contrasts: a search in the wilderness, a moment charged with divine intervention, and a ceremonial grandeur that seemed almost fragile under the weighty hopes of a nation longing for security and identity. The story of his rise is as much about the people as it is about the man himself. This social milieu—Israel poised on the cusp of monarchy—envelopes Saul's journey, weaving tension and expectation into every step he takes from the fields to the royal throne. On the surface, Saul was inconspicuous. He did not boast an impressive pedigree beyond being the son of Kish, a man of some standing in the tribe of Benjamin but far from the elite lineage one might expect for a king. His physical stature was commanding; he stood head and shoulders above his contemporaries—a man both humble and imposing in appearance. In the daily rhythms of rural life, Saul displayed no extraordinary signs of future greatness. His initial role was modest—caring for his father's donkeys—yet this mundane task would soon become the gateway to an extraordinary destiny. The catalyst for Saul's transformation was a moment of urgent necessity: the donkeys wandered from Kish's possession, lost somewhere in the highlands. The loss itself might have been a trivial matter—commonplace in a time when herding and animal husbandry were part of survival—but to Saul, it posed a deeper personal challenge. It was this search that led him out of his familiar boundaries and into the company of the prophet Samuel, setting in motion a divine plan that neither Saul nor the people around him fully comprehended at the time. Samuel's role in this narrative was both politically revolutionary and spiritually weighty. As the last of the judges and a prophet of God, Samuel carried the immense responsibility of leading Israel through social instability and preparing the people for monarchy—a concept that was simultaneously glorious and fraught with risk. Under his guidance, the nation had cried out for a king to lead them "like all the nations" (1 Samuel 8:5), yet the very idea of a monarch was a leap into unknown territory, a surrender of the direct divine rule that had defined their identity for centuries. When Saul arrived to meet Samuel, the prophet had already been divinely instructed to anoint the future king. The setting was intimate, something between the pastoral simplicity of village life and the solemnity of sacred ritual. Samuel's initial assessment of Saul was telling: the young man was tall, handsome, and physically impressive, qualities that drew favorable attention from the elders and the people present. But as Samuel warned, appearance alone was not the measure of a king; inner character mattered most. The anointing ceremony itself was unlike any Israelite ritual before—a public, religious, and political event rolled into one. Samuel took a vial of sacred oil and poured it over Saul's head, a symbolic act of consecration and empowerment. This moment marked not just the designation of a leader but the consecration of a new order under God's sovereignty filtered through human authority. The oil, thick and fragrant, seeped into Saul's hair and skin like the embodiment of divine blessing and commission. In the immediate aftermath, Saul's reaction was a mix of humility and bewilderment. He had not sought greatness; rather, it had found him. This humility, partly genuine and partly born of uncertainty, was essential to the early years of his reign and reflected the tentative nature of the monarchy's foundation. The people around Saul, too, were both excited and uncertain. Here was a tall, handsome man from their own tribe, anointed by the prophet Samuel, bearing the weight of their collective hopes—and yet no one could predict the path that lay ahead. From the vantage point of Israel's cities and villages, the announcement of Saul as king carried the electric thrill of change. The tribal elders, who had long vied for influence, now grappled with a new figure whose authority was divinely sanctioned and politically decisive. A burgeoning sense of unity spread as the tribes gathered to acclaim Saul, an expression of their yearning for stability in the face of encroaching external threats. The presence of this united assembly invoked ancient memories of tribal gatherings in the sanctuary, binding the people together in a shared destiny. The coronation was more than a solemn act; it was a performance of national identity. The narrators of the time described how the Spirit of God came powerfully upon Saul after the anointing, equipping him for the tasks ahead. Witnesses to this spiritual transformation were awestruck, sensing that this moment transcended political expediency and touched the profound mystery of divine intervention. The Spirit's arrival elevated Saul from mere man to a vessel of God's purpose, temporarily cloaking him with wisdom and courage in extraordinary measure. Saul's initial acts as king were watched closely by all. His mission was to unify the twelve tribes, subdue Israel's enemies, and lead with justice and strength. The social fabric of Israel, composed of diverse and often fractious tribes, depended heavily on a king who could hold them together without fraying their internal autonomy. Saul's leadership style at first appeared promising, striking a delicate balance between authority and the people's expectations. Yet beneath the surface, the fragility of this new monarchy was palpable. The transition from judges to kings was fraught with tension—questioning voices lurked in the background, wary of losing their independence, skeptical of this "human king" replacing God's direct governance. There were murmurs of concern that the king might lead them into tyranny or war beyond their means. But for now, the hopes were higher than the doubts, and the people longed to believe in Saul's potential. The political landscape to which Saul was introduced was complex and volatile. His reign began amid real threats from surrounding nations such as the Philistines, Moabites, and Ammonites, each pressing on Israel's borders and testing the fragile unity he sought to forge. The call for a strong, centralized monarchy was as much a reaction to these external dangers as it was a response to inner divisions. Saul's military leadership was therefore expected not only to defend but to assert Israel's standing among the nations, signaling a new chapter of resilience and confidence. Socially, Saul's rise also signaled a subtle shift in the dynamics between rural and urban life. His origins as a man from the Benjaminite hills reminded many of Israel's agrarian roots, yet as king, he had to navigate the demands of burgeoning towns and sanctuaries, harnessing their resources and allegiances. This balancing act required astute diplomacy and a vision beyond mere military victories. He was tasked with integrating the old traditions with the new political realities, shaping an Israelite identity that could endure. The excitement among the people was tangible. When Saul was publicly declared king, there was celebration but also a cautious hopefulness, an awareness that the future was uncertain yet ripe with possibility. Prophetic voices endorsed him, the elders pledged allegiance, and the people tentatively embraced this new order. The ceremony and ensuing feasts were moments when the communal solidarity was most vividly displayed, as Israel collectively stepped into the light of monarchy for the first time. Yet, amidst the celebrations, an undercurrent of tension remained. Saul himself was aware of the immense responsibilities and the precariousness of his position. The weight of expectations must have pressed heavily upon him in those early days, as the eyes of the nation—and of God—watched closely. His ambivalence was not surprising; kingship was a mantle of glory but also a yoke of vulnerability. As Saul moved from the fields to the throne, he entered not only a new role but also a complex psychological terrain. His initial humility and openness to the Spirit of God would later be tested by the temptations of power, doubts, and personal failings. But at this opening chapter of his kingship, Saul symbolized hope—a bridge between the turbulent past and a future yet unwritten. This story of Saul's rise, rich in detail and spirit, is more than a historical account. It is a narrative laden with meaning for Israel and for any people poised at moments of profound change. Saul's journey from humble beginnings to crowned glory embodies the fragile promise of new beginnings—hope tinged with risk, the unpredictable interplay of divine will and human agency, and the eternal challenge of leadership. For Israel, this moment charted a course toward monarchy that would shape its destiny for centuries, a legacy inseparable from the figure of Saul, the anointed king who began it all.

The Crown's Weight: Early Challenges

The moment Saul stepped forward as the first anointed king of Israel, the weight of destiny settled heavily on his shoulders. No longer was he simply a man from the tribe of Benjamin, tall and handsome, standing out among his people. He was now the symbol of a nation yearning for unity and strength, the man whose fate was intertwined with Israel's future. The transition from tribal judges to a centralized monarchy brought with it exhilaration but also an immense burden—one that would test Saul's resolve in ways no one could have anticipated. At the outset of his reign,

Saul was met with a nation rife with internal divisions and external threats. The tribes of Israel, long accustomed to a decentralized form of leadership under judges, struggled to fully embrace the monarchic structure. As a ruler, Saul had to navigate these turbulent waters: forging alliances, asserting his authority, and confronting enemies that sought to exploit any sign of weakness. The early chapters of his kingship were charged with the kind of tension that comes from holding together a fragile and fractious people on the brink of transformation. One of the immediate challenges Saul faced was the aggressive threat from the Amalekites. The Amalekites had long been Israel's foes, raiding their lands and striking fear into the hearts of the people. In Saul's first military campaign, this threat became the crucible by which his kingship would be tested. The command from Samuel was clear and unequivocal: utterly destroy the Amalekites without exception—men, women, children, livestock—everything was to be wiped out in obedience to God's judgment upon this enemy. Saul assembled Israel's forces and descended upon the Amalekites, and initial victories seemed to affirm his leadership. The troops rallied behind their king, their hearts lifted by the prospect of security and deliverance. But beneath the surface of triumph, cracks began to form. Saul spared King Agag alive, and he allowed the best of the sheep and cattle to live, rationalizing that these could be sacrificed as offerings to God. At first glance, these decisions might have appeared pragmatic or even pious, but their consequences would prove far-reaching. The episode revealed a profound tension between Saul's personal judgment and the divine command entrusted to him. When Samuel confronted Saul, accusing him of disobedience despite seeming success, Saul responded defensively, insisting his partial obedience was better than outright failure. Yet Samuel's grief was palpable, a stark reminder that in the emerging monarchy, the king's power was not absolute; it was subject to the higher authority of God. "To obey is better than sacrifice," Samuel declared, underscoring the principle that loyalty to God's word must supersede expediency. This moment echoed throughout Saul's reign, setting a pattern of conflict between divine will and human calculation. Saul's leadership, marred by this early lapse, would struggle under the double pressure of maintaining royal authority and walking in faithful obedience. The tension between these demands began to shape the king's character and decision-making, often with devastating results. Amid these military struggles, Saul contended with a delicate political landscape. The tribes, while united under his kingship, bore the scars of historic divisions and fiercely guarded their particular privileges and autonomy. Saul's own tribe of Benjamin was small and relatively weak, and his elevation to king stirred both hope and envy across Israel. Some factions questioned his legitimacy, while others awaited signs of strength and wisdom. Saul's challenge was to solidify his throne by winning the loyalty of these disparate groups, balancing firmness with favor, and making alliances that would ensure the new monarchy's survival. This political balancing act was complicated by Saul's growing insecurities and occasional impulsiveness. Early successes bred both confidence and paranoia. The king's desire to please his people and secure his reign pushed him to make decisions that often revealed his inexperience. For example, his premature offering of the burnt sacrifice before a battle, an act reserved for the prophet Samuel, reflected a fragile grasp of his royal role and relationship to God. When Samuel arrived and rebuked him, the humiliation deepened Saul's internal turmoil, casting long shadows over his sovereignty. Throughout these tumultuous events, Samuel remained a crucial figure—not only as a prophet but also as a counselor and spiritual guide. His presence anchored the nascent monarchy to its divine foundation. Samuel's role was complex; he was both the anointer of the king and the voice of God's judgment, which sometimes put him at odds with Saul's ambitions. His impartiality and insistence on covenantal faithfulness introduced a moral gravity that often highlighted the king's shortcomings. Samuel's guidance in the early years of Saul's reign was both stabilizing and tense. He called the king to repentance when needed and offered counsel grounded in divine wisdom. Yet the prophet's growing awareness of Saul's flaws—in obedience, temperament, and leadership—foreshadowed the difficulties ahead.

These interactions were laced with a mixture of mentorship and reproach—a dynamic that underscored the fragile relationship between God's messenger and the chosen earthly ruler. The tension of loyalty played out on many levels. Tribal leaders, military commanders, and common citizens watched Saul's reign with a cautious eye. Were his actions those of a true deliverer of Israel, or would the monarchy falter under inexperience and human frailty? The uncertainty bred factions and whispered dissent, as the king's counselors jockeyed for favor and influence. Each military victory was a cause for celebration, but each misstep quickly became fodder for criticism. One particularly vivid episode that captures the precarious nature of Saul's leadership is the conflict with the Philistines—a formidable foe whose military superiority challenged the very existence of Israel. As Saul prepared his men for battle, the anxiety among the soldiers mounted. Their weapons were inferior; their numbers, fewer. They looked to their king not only for tactical command but for inspiration and reassurance. Yet Saul's earlier mistakes and moments of hesitation sowed doubt, even among his closest followers. Time and again, Saul's decisions on the battlefield revealed the delicate balance he struggled to maintain: the need to act boldly and swiftly against external threats, while also managing the internal cohesion of his forces. When battles went against his expectations, his anxiety intensified, laying bare the immense pressure he bore. This pressure was compounded by the growing complexity of his role—he was no longer a tribal leader or judge but a king, expected to embody national unity, divine favor, and martial prowess. Samuel's role during these periods of crisis was particularly poignant. As a prophet, he was the conduit through whom God's will was communicated, often delivering hard truths to the king. Samuel's visits to the camp, his instructions, and his public declarations served both to support and to challenge Saul. The prophet insisted on obedience to God's commands as essential for victory and legitimacy. When Saul failed in this respect, Samuel's disappointment was public and profound. The prophet's withdrawal from the king's court marked a turning point, signaling a waning divine endorsement that weighed heavily on Saul's reign. Behind the headlines of wars and political maneuvering lie moments captured in the daily rhythms of court life—moments revealing Saul's humanity amid the grandeur of kingship. His private struggles with self-doubt, his desire to please his people, and his fear of losing legitimacy were real and raw. Accounts of his interactions with his son Jonathan show the warmth and vulnerability beneath the armor of monarchy, hinting at a man deeply aware of the stakes but uncertain in his own footing. The early years of Saul's reign, therefore, were a fraught mixture of hope and foreboding. Victory in battle brought cheers, but often it was followed by the somber reflection of unfulfilled promises and divine disappointment. The king's initial decisions—both on the battlefield and in political dealings—not only shaped the immediate fate of Israel but foreshadowed the eventual unraveling of his kingship. In examining these turbulent days, the complexity of the transition from judges to monarchy becomes clear. Saul's reign was not a simple story of success or failure but a nuanced unfolding of leadership under divine scrutiny. The exhilaration of being Israel's first king was inextricably woven with the precariousness of wielding power without full mastery. His reign captured the hopes of a nation but also the dangers inherent when a man grapples with a destiny larger than himself. Through it all, Samuel's ever-watchful presence framed the narrative as a reminder that true authority stems from obedience and faithfulness—not merely from royal decree or military might. The prophet's role as counselor and spiritual authority challenged Saul's every move, underscoring the fragile alliance between divine will and human governance. The crown Saul wore was, from the beginning, no simple ornament of power. It was a heavy burden, pressing down with the demands of war, politics, faith, and legacy. Each decision weighed not only on the king's immediate circumstances, but carried the weight of Israel's hopes and future. As Saul stood at the dawn of his reign, the early challenges he confronted painted a vivid portrait of a leader struggling to bear the crown's weight—a narrative defined by both the promise of a united Israel and the shadows of human frailty growing ever longer.

Saul's Spiritual Decline

The initial days of Saul's reign were marked by promise and the eager hope of a nation newly united under a single monarch. Samuel, the prophet who had anointed him as king, remained a guiding presence, a bridge between Saul and the divine will. Yet beneath the surface of triumph and national celebration, the seeds of spiritual unraveling were quietly taking root. This subchapter seeks to explore those darkening moments, when Saul's heart veered from obedience toward doubt, fear, and pride—and with it, began a tragic estrangement from the very source of his authority and blessing. Saul's decline was not abrupt; it emerged gradually, a slow corrosion of faith under pressure, a fragile confidence buckling before the heavy weight of kingship and expectation. The mantle of leadership, immense and unwieldy, revealed a character both noble and fractured. His initial zeal, a fiery devotion to God and country, was soon tempered—and then twisted—by a restless spirit and growing insecurity. The turning point came during a critical juncture in Saul's reign—a moment when obedience to God's command was demanded without hesitation or compromise. Samuel had given Saul precise instructions regarding the Amalekites, the sworn enemies of Israel, a people whose destruction was decreed by divine command as a judgment upon their long-standing hostility and sin. This command was absolute: "Now go and attack Amalek, and utterly destroy all that they have, and do not spare them; but kill both man and woman, infant and nursing child, ox and sheep, camel and donkey." Saul led his army with fervor and achieved a great victory, striking fear into the hearts of surrounding nations. But it was in the aftermath that fragility cracked the facade of his kingship. Instead of following Samuel's ordained command to the letter, Saul spared Agag, the Amalekite king, and kept the best of the livestock under the pretext that those animals would be sacrificed to the Lord. This disobedience, whether rationalized or born from an inner wavering, was the first clear fissure between Saul's will and God's instructions. When Samuel confronted Saul, the tension was palpable, a confrontation not merely of words but of hearts. "Why have you not obeyed the voice of the Lord?" Samuel demanded, voice heavy with prophetic authority. Saul's response was defensive, tipping into evasion, "I have obeyed the Lord; I have gone the way which the Lord sent me, and have brought Agag the king of Amalek, and have utterly destroyed the Amalekites. But the people took of the spoil, sheep and oxen, the chief of the things which should have been utterly destroyed, to sacrifice to the Lord your God in Gilgal." The prophet's rebuke cut deep. "Has the Lord as great delight in burnt offerings and sacrifices, as in obeying the voice of the Lord? Behold, to obey is better than sacrifice, and to heed than the fat of rams." Saul's spiritual decline deepened here, in this moment of confrontation—this collision of human pride with divine mandate. His failure was not simply in the spared king or the livestock; it was his failure to trust completely in God's authority, to surrender his own judgment for the sake of obedience. Pride had clouded his heart, his vanity insisting that he knew best, that his own logic could supplant divine command. The very act of sparing the best animals, under the guise of sacrifice, was a cruelty to obedience rather than a reverence for God. From this point forward, Samuel informed him that the Lord had rejected him as king. This pronouncement was a death knell—not just politically, but spiritually. The presence that had once anointed Saul, the Spirit of the Lord that had empowered him in decisive moments, would soon depart. As Samuel left Saul that day, a deep sadness filled the air. The gulf between prophet and king widened, one irreparably breached by disobedience and distrust. Samuel's grief was visceral; Israel had lost a leader, but Saul had lost God's favor, the lifeblood of true kingship. The story of Saul's decline is not merely a biblical recounting of error, but a timeless portrait of the human heart wrestling with power, fear, and the seduction of self. In the following days, the dissolution of Saul's favor manifested in more visible ways. The Spirit of the Lord, once a fierce and steady presence upon him, departed, and in its place came what the text calls an "evil spirit from the Lord," a troubling force that tormented Saul's mind and soul. This spiritual torment symbolizes the internal chaos ripping through the king's being—a clash between the divine purpose for which he was made and the brokenness of his own choices. It was during this dark season that David, the young shepherd boy and future king, entered Saul's court, initially as a musician to soothe the king's anguished spirit. David's rise only emphasized Saul's spiraling insecurity, fueling a paranoia that would ultimately consume him. The once confident king now found himself tormented by jealousy and suspicion, fearing David's growing popularity and favor with the people and the Lord. This fear exacerbated Saul's internal tumult, turning toward outward acts of cruelty and rashness. The man who was once anointed by the Spirit, leading armies and rallying a nation, was now driven by suspicion to plot murder against the very young man who brought him peace. Where obedience and faith once shone, fear and wounded pride now festered. One vivid scene captures this tragic transformation: Saul, in a fit of desperation and rage, attempted to kill David with a spear. David evaded the blow, and the king's rage only intensified. This was no longer the confident, prudent leader anointed by Samuel but a man tormented by inner demons, a king losing hold of both his sanity and his divine mandate. Moreover, Saul's spiritual decline extended to the point where he sought forbidden counsel. When the Philistine threat loomed, and Samuel was nowhere to be found, Saul turned to the witch of Endor, secretly seeking guidance from the dead prophet. This act was the final breach—desperation leading him into occult practices forbidden by God and a stark admission of his isolation and doubt.

Saul's disobedience had turned to desperation, highlighting the tragic void at the heart of his kingship. Through Saul's story, the themes of pride and fear, obedience and doubt play out with devastating effect. His royal stature, once radiant and promising, stood in harsh contrast to the inner spiritual decay. The grandeur of his title and the weight of a nation's hopes only underscored the tragedy of a soul slipping away from divine favor. In the silence left by Saul's withdrawal, a new hope was quietly rising in the figure of David, a young shepherd chosen to replace a fallen king. But the emotional gravity of Saul's fall remains heavy—a reminder that the blessing of God is not a guarantee but a fragile trust, one sustained by obedience, humility, and faith. Saul's spiritual decline is thus a tragic, poignant chapter in Israel's history. It exposes the tension between human ambition and divine will, between the search for personal glory and the call to humble service. His story compels the reader to confront the consequences of pride unchecked by faith, of fear masquerading as wisdom, and of a heart estranged from God's presence. The narrative invites us not only to witness Saul's collapse but to empathize with a man caught between his destiny and his flaws. His failure reverberates beyond history, into the realm of timeless human experience—the painful distance between what could have been and what was allowed to slip away. Ultimately, the tale of Saul's spiritual decline offers a vivid tableau of a king's tragic fall—and warns of the peril when the crown outruns the character, when divine favor is exchanged for the fleeting solace of fear and self-will. It is a cautionary story of lost grace, a compelling blend of history and humanity that continues to stir hearts and minds long after the echoes of his reign have faded.

Prophetic Judgment and Farewell

The twilight of Samuel's relationship with Saul marks one of the most heartrending and theologically profound moments in biblical history. As the first king of Israel, Saul was God's anointed instrument—a vessel chosen to bring about the unity and strength that the nation desperately needed at the dawn of the monarchy. Yet, his reign faltered under the burdens of pride, disobedience, and human frailty. It is within this somber context that the prophet Samuel steps forward to deliver the divine verdict—a decisive and sorrow-laden pronouncement that echoes through the generations. The scene is set amid a nation at a crossroads. The initial hope and fervor that accompanied Saul's coronation have waned. The people, who once hailed him with jubilation, have begun to experience the consequences of a king who, despite early promise, has failed to embody the covenantal ethos expected of Israel's monarchy. The prophetic word from Samuel cuts through the clamor, unflinching and clear: God has rejected Saul as king. This rejection is not a mere political dismissal but a profound spiritual severing, a divine judgment underscored by deep sorrow and inevitability. As Samuel gathers the people, the atmosphere pulsates with a heavy sense of finality. The prophet's voice, once brimming with zeal and hope, now carries the weight of a mournful burden. His words convey not only the judgment against Saul, but a lament for what might have been—a future lost to wrongful choices and moral compromise. The very air seems to thicken with the tension between justice and compassion, the sacred tension that governs the relationship between the Divine and humanity. Samuel's pronouncement is more than a historical verdict; it is a theological declaration about the nature of kingship, divine authority, and human responsibility. The rejection of Saul serves as a solemn lesson: God's anointing is not a guarantee of unending favor but a sacred trust that demands obedience and humility. Saul's failures epitomize the dangers of arrogance and disobedience, reminding the Israelite community that leadership in God's chosen nation is not about power or personal gain but about faithfulness to covenantal law. In this moment, Samuel embodies the prophetic office in its fullest dimensions. He is the messenger of God's judgment, the spokesman for divine will, but he is also a mourner grieving the consequences of human sin. His voice bridges heaven and earth, authority and compassion, justice and sorrow. The prophetic judgment he proclaims is irrevocable, yet it is delivered with a palpable sense of heartbreak—an acknowledgment of human weakness and the tragic unfolding of history. Throughout this farewell to Saul, the legacy of Samuel's own prophetic mission shines with clarity. From the early days of his calling, Samuel had been a beacon of divine guidance and moral clarity in a tumultuous era. His life and ministry reveal the profound challenge of faithful leadership in a fallen world—a world where even the anointed can fall, where the line between success and failure is often perilously thin. Samuel's farewell underscores the paradox of prophecy:

the calling to speak truth to power, even when that truth brings pain and division. The pronouncement against Saul also signals a pivotal transition for Israel. It foreshadows the coming rise of David, the shepherd king whose heart aligned more closely with God's purposes. Yet, the shift from Saul's failed kingship to David's eventual reign is not presented as simple or smooth. Rather, it unfolds within the complex realities of political intrigue, personal rivalries, and divine providence. Samuel's prophecy thus serves as both an end and a beginning—a closing chapter on one era and the herald of another. Reflections on divine justice permeate this moment. God's rejection of Saul is not arbitrary but rooted in a covenantal relationship that demands faithfulness. It reveals the holy seriousness of divine expectations and the consequences when those expectations are unmet. Samuel's role as a prophet reveals the often painful interface between divine will and human action, reminding readers that judgment is never easy, nor is it devoid of love. Embedded in this judgment is also a stark acknowledgment of human frailty. Saul's story is a tragic narrative of potential unfulfilled, a cautionary tale about the seductions of power and the perils of disobedience. Samuel's mourning communicates a deep empathy for the human condition—an understanding that leaders, no less than ordinary people, are vulnerable to weakness, failure, and the consequences of their choices. This balance of judgment and compassion lends profound depth to the prophetic tradition. The final arc of this chapter culminates in Samuel's farewell, imbued with a sense of both closure and solemn hope. He departs from the public stage, but the prophetic torch is never extinguished. The mantle is passed—not only to David but to the enduring role of the prophet in holding kings accountable, ensuring that divine justice remains central in the life of the nation. Samuel's farewell, then, is both an ending and a promise: that God's purposes, though often delayed and complicated, will ultimately prevail. In these closing moments, the interplay between divine sovereignty and human agency crystallizes. Samuel's authority as a prophet is both a gift and a heavy burden. He must announce God's judgment, bear the sorrow of rejection, and yet remain steadfast in the assurance that God's plan moves forward. The text invites readers to grapple with these tensions—the discomfort of divine judgment coupled with the hope of renewal. Through the lens of Samuel's prophetic judgment and farewell, the reader is invited to confront timeless themes relevant to leadership, faith, and the consequences of human action. The personal drama of Saul's collapse is a mirror reflecting broader spiritual truths: the imperative of obedience, the dangers of pride, the cost of turning away from God's commands. Samuel's example as a prophet offers a model of courageous faithfulness, even when the prophetic word cuts deep and comes at great personal cost. This narrative also serves as a meditation on legacy—both the legacy we leave through our actions and the legacy bestowed upon us through divine purpose. Samuel's own life embodies this dual legacy: a man chosen from boyhood, nurtured in the temple, raised as God's servant, who must now grapple with the failure of the king he once anointed. His legacy is one of steadfast devotion, prophetic integrity, and unwavering commitment to God's will, a legacy that underscores the sacred responsibility that accompanies leadership. Ultimately, the prophetic judgment against Saul and Samuel's farewell are a testament to the complex relationship between God's sovereignty and human leadership—a relationship marked by grace, justice, sorrow, and hope. It is a solemn call to vigilance for all who bear authority, a reminder that true leadership is measured not by strength or popularity but by fidelity to divine purpose. As the chapter closes, the reader is left with the resonant image of Samuel standing at the precipice of history, his heart heavy but his vision clear, bearing the weight of God's word as Israel awaits the dawn of a new king. This moment, at once a requiem and a prologue, encapsulates the enduring power of prophecy and the unyielding hope that in God's hands, even failure can be transformed into the foundation for new beginnings.

The Shepherd and the Ages: The Advent of David

Finding the Hidden Shepherd

The sun hung low in the western sky, casting a golden glow over the rolling hills of Bethlehem. Shadows stretched lazily across the patchwork of olive groves and vineyards, weaving intricate patterns on the earth. A gentle breeze stirred, carrying with it the faint scent of wild thyme and freshly turned soil, mingling with the unmistakable aroma of grazing sheep. In this quiet tableau, the world seemed untouched by the weight of destiny—as if time itself had paused, allowing nature's rhythm to unfold unhindered. Amid the soft murmur of bleating sheep and the crunch of hoofbeats on dry grass, a solitary figure moved thoughtfully among the flock.

David, the youngest son of Jesse, was a young shepherd boy whose days were spent in the honest companionship of his sheep. His frame was slender, his hands calloused but deft, accustomed to wielding sling and staff alike. His eyes, a clear and bright brown, scanned the horizon with a mix of vigilance and tranquility that spoke of years spent alone in these fields, pondering the mysteries of life under the vast desert sky. This pastoral scene, simple and unassuming, was about to become the very stage upon which one of Israel's greatest divine dramas would unfold. Yet, in this moment, no one could guess that this boy—scraping a stray burr from a woolly ram's shoulder, humming a soft melody learned from the elders—was destined to become the chosen king of Israel. The hidden shepherd, obscured amidst the hills and olive trees, was about to be found. Far from Bethlehem, the prophet Samuel journeyed with a determined pace, his heart heavy but resolute. The words of the Lord had come clearly in the night, cutting through sleep like a blade: "Samuel, the Lord has rejected Saul as king over Israel. Rise and anoint for me a man from

Bethlehem, from the clan of Jesse, for I have provided myself a king." The divine command was unmistakable, yet its fulfillment lay shrouded in mystery. Samuel's path led him across the rugged terrain of Judah, through groves kissed by the setting sun and fields swaying with barley ready for harvest. Each step seemed weighted by the burden of judgment and hope intertwining within his soul. The air, tinged with the dust of distant roads, carried the faint sounds of village life—the laughter of children playing near stone huts, the soft bleating of sheep gathered for evening rest, the distant call of a watchman winding down the day's vigil. Arriving at the outskirts of Bethlehem, Samuel paused. The town's modest structures were nestled like scattered jewels upon the hillside, their whitewashed walls glowing warmly in the twilight. Olive trees—ancient and gnarled—stood sentinel over the landscape, their leaves shimmering silver beneath the dying light. Here was a place where the rhythm of life had changed little over the years, where stories of old mingled with the daily toil of farmers and shepherds. Samuel's eyes swept the countryside, settling on a nearby hillside where a flock grazed peacefully. There, a boy moved among sheep with practiced ease, his voice rising in soft songs carried aloft on the gentle breeze. In this humble act—nurturing and protecting the flock—was a quiet nobility that belied his youth. As the prophet approached the encampment of Jesse's family, the rustic sounds of the evening cocooned him—the crackle of a small fire, the occasional bark of a dog, a low murmur of voices blending with the chirping of crickets. In these simple surroundings, the cosmic weight of kings and kingdoms seemed almost incongruous. Upon meeting Jesse's sons, Samuel carefully regarded each—Eliab, the eldest, tall and commanding with his broad shoulders and earnest gaze; Abinadab, strong and quiet; Shammah, a figure of steady presence; and the younger ones, each displaying traits of potential leadership and might. Yet, as the prophet looked upon them under the fading light, none stirred within him the certainty of God's choice. The tension in Samuel's heart tightened. The search had brought him here, yet the hidden king remained unseen. The weight of divine expectation settled heavily on his shoulders; the air seemed charged with the silent question: Who among these men would bear the mantle of Israel's future? Then, as the household began to wonder if the moment had passed, the youngest son was summoned from the fields. David, still dusted with the earth of pasture and sun-warmed olive groves, stepped forward—not with the boldness of a warrior, but with a quiet dignity shaped by years of solitude and shepherd's service. His skin bore the subtle tan of outdoor labor, his eyes glimmering with humility and an unspoken strength. The scent of his cloak, faintly mingled with herbs and the faintest trace of sheep's wool, carried the essence of a life lived close to the land. The air around him seemed to shift, as if the earth itself recognized the presence of one chosen. Samuel's hand trembled slightly as he lifted the sacred horn filled with oil. The last rays of sunlight filtered through the olive branches, casting a celestial glow around the boy who knelt before him. In this act, both simple and profound, the hidden shepherd—David—was revealed as the one the Lord had ordained. The pastoral tranquility of that evening masked a monumental transition. The simple melodies sung among the fields, the rustic textures of bark and stone, the warmth of sun and soil—all converged to bear witness to the birth of a new chapter in Israel's history. The boy who tended sheep under endless skies was, in divine purpose, stepping into a role that would redefine not just a kingdom, but a people's destiny. As twilight deepened and stars began to prick the velvet sky, the reverberations of that moment echoed silently across the hills. From the innocence of the shepherd's world emerged the weighty mantle of kingship, resting now upon David's shoulders. And though the path ahead would be marked by trials, triumphs, and profound transformation, on this day, in the fading light of Bethlehem's fields, the hidden shepherd was finally found.

The Anointing in Secret

The olive grove was quiet, the heavy boughs of ancient trees casting long shadows in the fading light—shadows that seemed to ripple and dance with secrets whispered only to the wind. Beneath this canopy, far from the watchful eyes of men and the scrutinizing gaze of the court, a moment of profound significance unfolded, destined to alter the course of Israel's history. It was here, concealed by nature's embrace and the stillness of evening, that Samuel, God's chosen prophet, carried out the anointing of a young shepherd boy named David—an event as clandestine as it was momentous. The sun had dipped low beyond the hills of Bethlehem, staining the sky with hues of crimson and gold, when Samuel arrived. His steps were measured, his demeanor solemn yet charged with quiet urgency. This was no ordinary gathering, no public ceremony full of grandeur and trumpets. The anointing was to be a secret kept beneath the sacred veil of darkness, a sacred rite known by only a handful—an intimate covenant forged between the divine and mortal realms. David, the youngest son of Jesse, stood nervously among his older brothers, their robust frames stark against his slight figure and ruddy complexion. They were gathered for what seemed a routine family visit by the prophet, but David alone bore the unspoken weight of destiny—a weight invisible yet unmistakably present. Though he was unknown to the wider world, his heart was attuned to something greater, something beyond the pastures and sheepfolds where he had spent his days. Samuel's eyes met David's with an intensity that cut through the evening's stillness. There was recognition there—an acknowledgment whispered by God Himself. Slowly, the prophet reached into his satchel and withdrew the small horn of oil, its contents a sacred liquid imbued with divine purpose. The oil's golden sheen caught the last of the light, glistening as liquid sunlight poured from the heavens. The ceremony began in hushed tones. No words of fanfare or elevation echoed here—only the soft murmur of prayer and invocation, a sacred dialogue conducted between the heavens and the earth. Samuel's voice was both a whisper and a reality, powerful yet gentle: a call to the Spirit to descend, to consecrate, and to mark a vessel for a destiny yet unseen. David's hands trembled slightly as Samuel lifted the horn and tipped the oil upon his head. The warm liquid trickled down, a tangible symbol of divine favor, a spiritual anointment sealing

David's role as God's chosen instrument. It was not merely a ritual; it was a moment of transformation—a redefinition of identity and purpose. To the untrained eye, the boy might have appeared unchanged. But beneath the skin, within the marrow of his being, something had been awakened. The oil was a silent anointing of revelation and courage, strength and humility, a divine empowerment that would sustain him through trials no earthly armor could withstand. The secret nature of the ceremony held immense significance. It was necessary that this event unfold without public knowledge, for in the shadowed corridors of power, intrigue and jealousy stirred like restless serpents. To anoint David openly before the current king, Saul, would have invited conflict and premature peril. The hidden anointing was a divine decree protected from human machinations, a sacred trust preserved until the appointed time. This concealment also carried a deeper esoteric meaning. It reflected the spiritual truth that God's sovereign work often unfolds in obscurity before bursting into the light. True authority and destiny are nurtured quietly, in hidden chambers of the soul, through unseen grace rather than worldly acclaim. As the last drop of oil soaked into David's thick hair, the olive trees seemed to exhale, their leaves shimmering with an almost celestial glow. The air carried an intangible electricity, a mingling of the earthly and the holy. Samuel stepped back, his eyes alight with solemn joy and awe. A prophet's burden, heavy yet wondrous, rested now upon this humble shepherd boy. No fanfare followed. No herald announced the anointed king in waiting. Instead, there was only a reverent silence, the kind that speaks louder than words, a sacred pause pregnant with promise and quiet power. David was left to carry this secret within him, a divine spark ignited in the silence, waiting patiently beneath the surface of his daily life. He would return to his flocks, to the simple rhythms of shepherding, concealing the anointed destiny that crowned him far beyond the green pastures. This moment—the anointing in secret—served as a prophetic beacon, a fulcrum between the twilight of Saul's reign and the dawn of a new kingdom. It was both a safeguard and a declaration, a quiet yet profound testament to how God's purposes surpass human understanding and timing. In the unfolding years, the memory of this hidden rite would be a wellspring of strength for David. When he faced Goliath's taunts, the jeers of courtiers, and the treacheries of royal intrigues, the sacred oil poured in this olive grove would sustain him. It would be a spiritual armor, a reminder of destiny chosen in quiet faithfulness rather than public acclaim. The anointing was also a symbolic renewal of Israel's identity itself. David was not merely a boy; he was the embodiment of God's promise to establish a dynasty through a man after His own heart. The secret oil spoke of a future where leadership would be both divine and human, where the ruler would be a servant, and where the kingdom's foundation would be built on covenant faithfulness, courage, and divine guidance. This clandestine ceremony beneath the olives encapsulated the paradox of David's journey—the humility of a shepherd destined to be king, the invisibility of God's calling before its revelation, and the mysterious ways divine purpose often manifests in the ordinary. It was a moment suspended in time, a spiritual fulcrum on which the fate of Israel would turn. As the darkness deepened, Samuel departed quietly, leaving behind the silent witness of the ancient trees and the boy who carried God's anointing in secret. The path ahead was fraught with hardship, shadowed by the looming presence of Saul's fading kingship and the uncertainties of a kingdom in turmoil. Yet, within David burned a light kindled by that secluded pouring of oil, a light that would one day illuminate the nation's destiny and echo through the ages. Thus, in the covert anointing beneath the olive boughs, the hidden hand of God was revealed—not in spectacle, but in sacred silence. It was a moment that transcended the visible, a secret ripple sent through the spiritual fabric of Israel, quietly heralding the birth of a king unlike any before him, and the dawn of a new era in the life of a people chosen by God.

David's Early Years at Court

In the golden light of the early morning, the palace of King Saul stirred with a quiet energy—a tension barely concealed beneath the rituals of court life. It was within these walls, centuries old and shaped by countless events both grand and tragic, that David took his tentative first steps into a world vastly different from the quiet solitude of his father's fields. The journey from shepherd to courtier was not only a passage of geography but a profound crossing of cultures, expectations, and destinies. It would test his wisdom, courage, and heart in ways he had yet to fathom. David's arrival at the royal court was met with a swirl of reactions, each more revealing than the last. King Saul, the anointed first monarch of Israel, was a man of imposing stature and brooding temperament—complex in his emotions, torn between pride and unease. When Samuel's appointed anointed one first entered the court, Saul's gaze lingered on the young shepherd boy with an inscrutable mixture of curiosity and suspicion. "Who is this boy that plays the harp so sweetly?" inquired Abner, Saul's captain, during a hurried moment in the king's chambers. His voice was low but edged with the unmistakable scent of intrigue." David, the son of Jesse," Saul replied, fingers still trembling slightly from the sudden, unfathomable relief that had washed over him since David's first tones had soothed his torment. "The prophet Samuel sent him to us. It seems the Lord is not finished with this child yet." Yet beneath the official approval lay a simmering storm of emotions. Saul, feeling the heavy weight of his kingship, was no stranger to insecurity. The young David, celebrated for his bravery and favored by the people, was quickly woven into the tapestry of court life—his presence both balm and challenge. The court itself was a microcosm of a fledgling nation wrestling with its identity. Noblemen harbored ambitions delicate and dangerous; spies embedded in every conversation; women whispered in shadows, plotting alliances and protections. Into this intricate dance stepped David, a simple shepherd with the spirit of a lion, yet cautious as a fox, learning to navigate the labyrinthine politics of a kingdom in flux. David's first interactions with Saul's sons—Jonathan and Ish-bosheth—were telling. Jonathan, the heir apparent and a valiant warrior, was drawn to David with the depth of brotherly affection, recognizing a kindred spirit in courage and integrity. "You are more noble to me than ten thousand sons," Jonathan once confessed, their hands clasped in solemn friendship beneath the canopy of the king's courtyard. But not all embraced David's ascendancy with open hearts. Ish-bosheth, younger and more volatile, eyed the shepherd boy with a bitterness that foreshadowed future conflicts. His jealousy was a shadow that stretched long through the halls of the palace, coloring many private conversations and secret meetings. David, however, was not unaware of the perilous ground upon which he stood. His humility was genuine, but so was his understanding of power's delicate balance. The harp that had once accompanied him under star-lit skies became an instrument of diplomacy and solace in the royal chambers. He played to lift Saul's spirits, to calm the unrestful king in moments of gnawing doubt. In these stolen hours, David's charm and skill earned him favor, yet each note was a careful step along the tightrope of court intrigue. One of the early legends of David's court life was his intimate counsel to Saul during moments of crisis. When the king was troubled by nightmares and the black tempest of despair, David's music was his only refuge. Yet more than that—David's counsel, grounded not only in spiritual insight but also in a rising wisdom beyond his years, began to command attention." You have the heart of a warrior and the soul of a poet, boy," remarked Ahitub, the priest, observing David in quiet reverence. "There is a destiny in your eyes that neither king nor prophet can ignore." Yet Saul's emotions fluctuated unpredictably. When news arrived of David's victory over Goliath, the giant Philistine who had taunted Israel for weeks, the court erupted with celebration. David's valor was undeniable; his faith undeniable. But within Saul's heart, the seed of suspicion was planted. The more David's reputation grew, the more Saul grappled with a turbulent mix of honor and envy. On a chilly evening, beneath the flickering torchlight of the great hall, the tension finally surfaced in a conversation between king and subject. "Tell me, David," Saul demanded, gaze piercing, "do you seek to take my throne with the same sword that felled Goliath?" David met the king's eyes, steady and unflinching. "My lord," he replied softly, "my only desire is to serve the Lord and protect His people. I am a servant, not a rival." But words alone could not quell the storm within Saul. The king's paranoia deepened as David's friendship with Jonathan flourished—a bond marked by loyalty and tragic potential." Be cautious of your friends, lad," Saul warned one dusk. "In this palace, even those closest can wield the sharpest knives." Despite Saul's warnings, David was welcomed into the royal tables, sharing in feasts and counsel. He learnt the nuances of court diplomacy—the subtle nods, the concealed insults, the alliances formed under the guise of friendship. In these moments, David's wisdom shone brightest. He was quick to understand not only what was spoken but what was left unsaid. His decisions reflected a maturity beyond his years, balancing the needs of surviving the court's treacherous currents with an unwavering commitment to his higher purpose. At another point, during a gathering of elders and military leaders, the matter of regional skirmishes was raised. Many advocated for aggressive retaliation against neighboring Amalekites. David, speaking with a calm authority, proposed a strategy that balanced strength with prudence. "We must not only fight with the sword," he said, "but with wisdom that preserves what we have and builds what is just."This counsel won him respect, though silently, doubt persisted among some of Saul's advisors. To a man uneasy with change and threatened by rising stars, David was both indispensable and dangerous. One cannot tell the story of David's early years at court without acknowledging the role of Michal, Saul's daughter. To many, their marriage was a political move intended to bind David more closely to the royal family. But to David, Michal was more than a political pawn—her love offered sanctuary amid uncertainty. Michal's presence softened the stark realities of court life. There were moments, hidden in private chambers, where the weight of future kingship slipped away and two young souls found respite. Her unwavering belief in David's destiny became a shield in harsh times.Yet even this relationship bore the marks of the palace's strife. Michal's father's growing suspicions cast shadows on their union, and whispered conversations in the corridors spoke of plots and betrayals. Amid all this, David also earned the loyalty of others—notably the group of mighty men, the elite warriors who would become his trusted companions. These fierce, battle-tested men saw in David not only a leader but a man who embodied the ideals they fought for: courage, justice, and faith. One such warrior, Abishai, once declared, "In all Israel there is no one like our lord David—he is both lion and shepherd; his heart beats for the people." David's relationship with these men was forged not merely through command but through shared trials. Their loyalty was a vital counterbalance to the growing hostilities he faced within the court and from Saul himself. But the undercurrents of suspicion and rivalry eventually erupted into conflict. Saul's erratic mood swings gave way to open hostility. The king's attempts to kill David forced the young hero into exile, transforming the once privileged courtier into a fugitive. Still, even in turmoil, David's early years at court had laid the foundation for a leadership that would redefine a nation. The palace, with its grandeur and deceit, had been David's crucible. Here, amidst admiration and suspicion, music and fear, friendship and rivalry, he learned the true cost of destiny. In the tapestry of Israel's history, these early days at Saul's court were but a prologue—a stirring prelude to the epic saga yet to unfold. Within these chambers and courts, where power and faith collided, David's journey from shepherd boy to the awaited king had begun in earnest.

Prophetic Portent in the Wilderness

Beneath an expansive sky, where the stars glittered like shards of ancient glass scattered across an immense velvet canvas, David found himself alone in the wilderness. The night air was cool and crisp, carrying with it the scent of sagebrush, cedar, and the distant pine groves whispering secrets to the wind. Around him, low hills rolled gently into the darkness, their silhouettes outlined by the flickering light of a solitary campfire. Here, in this quiet seclusion, far from the courts of kings and the clamor of men, the young shepherd was touched by a profound stillness—a silence pregnant with possibility and portent. The wilderness was more than just a refuge from the world's dangers and distractions; it was a crucible, shaping David's spirit and forging his character in ways the palace walls never could. Each night, he lay beneath the vast, indifferent star-strewn heavens, the wild expanse echoing both his solitude and the grandeur of the calling sealed upon his life. To some, this expanse might appear barren, even desolate, yet for David, it was alive with meaning—an open book written by the hand of God, pages turning in the flickering glow of his campfire. Here, the wilderness was a paradox. It was both harsh and merciful, a place where wild beasts prowled and yet where quiet holiness could be found. It mirrored the tension embedded deep within David's journey—the clash between raw, unyielding trial and the gentle, unseen hand of divine guidance. Each gust of wind rustling through the dry grasses seemed to carry a message, an invisible whisper urging him onward. It was a land of test and promise, a liminal space where boyhood faded into manhood, where fear met faith, and where uncertainty mingled with the emergence of destiny. David's heart stirred beneath the canopy of the night. With his thoughts adrift in the cosmic calm above, he traced constellations with his eyes—Orion's belt burning steady and bright, the Great Bear lumbering across the heavens, and the luminous band of the Milky Way stretching like a ribbon of light. These celestial lights, untouchable and eternal, seemed to guide him in a profound communion. They were silent witnesses to the story unfolding below, a story of a shepherd king not yet crowned, a prophet's anointed one not yet known to the world. Their eternal gleam cast a radiant glow on the path that stretched endlessly before him, a path both illuminated by divine promise and shadowed by impending trials. In the heart of the wilderness, life slowed to the rhythm of the elements. The crackle of firewood breaking into flame, the distant call of a night bird, the soft hum of the wind threading through the trees—all worked to sharpen David's senses and attune his soul to a higher cadence. Here, prayer and reflection became as natural as breathing, and with every whispered supplication, his spirit grew more rooted in trust. The wilderness allowed him not just to survive but to learn resilience—from the stoic oak bending beneath the wind's push, from the wildflowers that blossomed despite the thorny brush. Nature itself embodied a teaching, a sacred lesson in endurance and hope. The nights also bore with them a gentle tension, a quiet knowing that the tranquillity would not last forever. As the embers glowed low and the stars wheeled overhead, David wrestled inwardly with a tide of emotions. The peaceful silence was pierced intermittently by thoughts of the future's uncertainties, of the enemies that lurked just beyond distant hills, and the heavy mantle of responsibility lying ahead. This wilderness was a place not just for rest but for preparation—a forging ground where the spirit was tempered for battle and leadership. The solitude lent itself to a precious kind of self-awareness, revealing the fragile interlace of courage and doubt that defined his heart. The flickering campfire became a symbol in itself: a steady flame against the engulfing darkness, an emblem of warmth amidst cold uncertainty. Its unpredictable light mirrored the fluctuating fortunes of the man to whom God's hand had been extended. Like the fire, David's faith was a constant battle to remain alight; it required tending, patience, and devotion, never allowed to be smothered under the weight of despair or fear. This fragile glow was a testament to hope alive amidst wilderness trials—an offering to the divine promise whispered to him through prophetic dreams and which the prophet Samuel had sealed with holy anointment. Morning broke with a soft blush on the horizon, the cold breath of night receding as the sun's first rays touched the earth. The wilderness transformed in daylight—harsh and unforgiving yet spectacular in its beauty. Golden grasses swayed in a gentle breeze; the sharp angles of rocky outcrops caught the light; birds burst forth in a chorus that rang through the valleys. In the retreat of shadows, David felt renewed and equipped to face whatever lay ahead. Daylight brought clarity, revealing hidden paths and new challenges, but also reaffirmed the truths sown deep during the long hours of meditation beneath the stars.

Within this solitude, David meditated not only on the tangible tasks of survival but also on his divine calling. He pondered the burden and privilege of leadership, aware that the wilderness was but a prelude to the throne he was destined to inherit. The trials faced in these remote expanses were necessary for cultivating the empathy, strength, and humility that a king would require. He knew well the stories of his ancestors—of shepherds who rose to lead and heroes who were forged by hardship. His own story was weaving into that grand tapestry, one thread entwined with the sacred history of Israel itself. The wilderness, then, was no mere backdrop but a living entity in David's saga. It stood as metaphor for the spiritual journey—a crossing through dark places toward the light of fulfilled destiny, a passage marked by both divine test and intimate revelation. It reminded him that greatness was birthed in places far removed from pomp and power, in moments of quiet surrender beneath a star-strewn sky. As he lay beside the dying fire, gazing upward, David's soul embraced a profound certainty: that in the wilderness, amid silence and shadows, the voice of God was clearest. This prophetic portent, whispered in the hush of night and carved into the rugged landscape, would accompany David not only through the rough terrain of the desert but also through the storms of a nation's transformation. The wilderness was sanctuary and classroom, refuge and clarion call, teaching him the weight of destiny moderated by the grace of the divine. It was here that the shepherd became the instrument of a greater purpose, patiently waiting, preparing—as the stars above bore silent witness to the birth of a king.

Prophet and Kingmaker: Samuel's Solo Compass

The Burden of Divine Messenger

The night was thick with silence, a heavy stillness broken only by the occasional crackle of a dying campfire, its amber light flickering against the canvas of Samuel's solitary tent. All around him, the vastness of the desert stretched into shadowed infinity, an endless expanse that seemed to mirror the inner wilderness he navigated each time the divine voice stirred within. Beneath the celestial canopy, speckled with countless stars, Samuel sat alone, the weight of a world's destiny pressing down upon his shoulders. Yet it was not merely the magnitude of his task or the fate of kings that burdened him; it was the profound solitude of being the bearer of messages few wished to hear, a solitary channel through which God's will flowed—sometimes like streams of mercy, often like rivers of judgment. To be God's messenger was a sacred privilege, but it was never a gift granted without cost. Samuel's heart was a crucible where hope and despair commingled in relentless alchemy. When the divine call came, it was as if the very air around him thickened, and his senses sharpened to an almost painful acuity.

The rustling leaves, the shifting sands, the whispering wind—all became part of a chorus that only he could hear, the voice of the Almighty speaking, not in thunderous proclamations, but in quiet, piercing commands that demanded immediate and absolute obedience. It was in those moments, under the cold gaze of the stars and the blackened sweep of the night, that Samuel felt simultaneously chosen and utterly alone. The burden of the divine messenger was more than the words he conveyed; it was the living cost of their consequences. When Samuel faced Saul, chosen by God to be Israel's first king, he carried not only the anointing oil but the devastations to come—the king's pride, rebellion, and eventual rejection by God. When he anointed David, the shepherd boy destined for greatness yet mired in trials and bloodshed, it was with trembling hope intertwined with foreknowledge of shadows yet to fall. Samuel's role was to stand as the solitary bridge between God's will and human frailty, a place of exaltation, but also deep vulnerability. In many ways, Samuel's nights were unlike those of any other man. While the people rested in ignorance or comfort, he grappled with the echoes of prophecy, with silent visions that neither gave rest nor peace. The quiet hours bore witness to his wrestling with the divine dilemma—to speak the truth and risk exile in the hearts of men or to silence the message and betray the very God who entrusted him. Each night, the crackling campfire was both a companion and a witness, casting dancing shadows that seemed to mimic the turmoil within his soul. He felt the heat of the flames on his skin juxtaposed with the cold knowledge that his calling would isolate him from the easy warmth of human fellowship. His solitude was not merely physical but spiritual. The prophetic life demanded a unique kind of communion, one lived often between worlds. Samuel stood on the narrow ridge, balanced precariously between the will of God and the will of man. To the people, he was a judge and guide, a kingmaker whose word could elevate or dismantle thrones. Yet beneath the mantle of authority lay a man profoundly aware of his own fragility, a vessel vulnerable to the crushing weight of expectations. The divine voice was exhilarating and terrifying in equal measure, bringing clarity but also a piercing loneliness that no crown or accolade could ease. Often, Samuel would find himself enveloped in metaphors that carried the truth of his experience more fully than mere words ever could. His role was like that of a lightning rod, drawn irresistibly to the fierce storm of God's will—receiving the bolt that none else could bear, channeling its destructive power but standing firm despite the burning charge. At other times, he saw himself as a seed planted in rocky soil; though it bore fruit, roots must dig deep beneath harsh surfaces where no eye could see the silent struggle. The weight he carried was a divine paradox: strength born of surrender, peace born of pain, purpose traced with isolation. Yet there were moments when the burden felt as a mantle woven with grace—a heavy but sanctified garment. Samuel knew consolation came not in applause or acceptance but in the steady whisper of God's presence in his heart. Each dark night's vigil, each solitary journey to the sacred altar, renewed a covenant that transcended human understanding. The contact with the divine was sometimes a beacon of hope that lit the path through political turmoil and personal doubt. It was this deep current of faith that sustained him when the people's voices rose in rebellion or indifference, when kings he had anointed faltered, or when his own prayers seemed to hang unanswered in the cold air. Samuel's prophetic calling was intensely personal. It pierced his soul with a clarity that transcended time and space. His life was a continuous conversation between the finite and the infinite, between flesh and spirit, between the demands of the present and the promises of the eternal. This dialogue was lived out in sensory detail: the sharp chill of night air seeping through his cloak, the rough texture of worn leather under his fingers, the distant cry of an owl echoing in the desolate hills. Each sensation grounded the intangible realities he confronted, forging a bond between the celestial and the terrestrial. In this sacred solitude, Samuel often wrestled with the paradox of empowerment and isolation. His power was unmistakable—through his voice kings rose and fell, the nation bent its course around his decrees, and the unseen hand of God moved visibly in history. But this power was a double-edged sword that cut deep into his humanity. To be the bearer of unwelcome truths was to invite rejection and scorn; to stand as the moral compass was to carry the heavy burden of judgment not only upon others but also within himself. The aloofness imposed by his calling was a wall both protective and imprisoning. He was elevated, yet apart; revered, yet misunderstood. On nights when Samuel pondered the trajectory of his life, he sometimes imagined his prophetic role as a narrow, lonely ridge between two great cliffs. On one side were the soaring heights of divine expectation, where every word and action might reshape history; on the other, the abyss of human rebellion and failure, where kings he had chosen might descend into ruin. His steps had to be measured, deliberate—one misstep could plunge the nation into chaos or his own spirit into despair. The ridge was exhausting to traverse, and yet retreat was impossible. The calling had ensnared him irrevocably, wrapping him in solemn purpose. There was also a profound awareness in Samuel's heart that no mortal could share the fullness of his burden. The people saw the prophet standing strong, the judge dispensing wisdom, the kingmaker anointing rulers destined for glory. But behind the public visage was a well of private lament and prayer—hours spent crying out to God for mercy on a people slow to listen, for strength to persevere when the weight seemed unbearable. His nights alone were not just times of divine encounter but moments when the prophet's soul bled in silence, when his faith was tested against bitter realities. The metaphor of fire frequently came to Samuel in these reflections—not only the campfires that warmed his body but a spiritual flame that burned deep within. This fire both purified and consumed, a sacred blaze that called for unwavering devotion but spared no layer of pretense or weakness. His prophetic words often felt like sparks cast into dry tinder; some ignited transformation, while others met resistance and rejection, threatening to smother the flame. To sustain this fire required constant tending— prayer, fasting, meditation—rituals that nourished his spirit even as his flesh faltered. Throughout his ministry, Samuel lived the tension of being beloved by God but rejected by many in his people. This duality sharpened his awareness of the fragile interface between divine ideal and human reality. The kings he anointed—Saul, the embattled first monarch; David, the destined shepherd-king—each embodied the struggle between aspiration and failure that raised Samuel's prophetic mission to a new level of complexity. He was both participant and observer, bearing the pain of broken promises while holding fast to the vision of God's covenantal faithfulness. Samuel's life was also a testament to endurance in the face of spiritual solitude. Unlike earthly leaders surrounded by courtiers or advisors, he often stood alone in the presence of holy demand. The divine voice that called him forth was a constant companion but also a relentless revealer of truth that few were willing to face. There was no crowd to cheer the prophet when his words fell hard, no assembly to share the burdens of judgment. This isolation deepened his dependence on God as his sole refuge and strength. The sensory world around Samuel—night winds that whispered through olive branches, the cool touch of river water as he cleansed himself after prayer, the scent of incense rising from the altar—became woven into the fabric of his spiritual experience. These tangible details rooted his intangible calling in the reality of lived time and space, offering moments of solace amid relentless responsibility. The interplay of light and shadow, sound and silence, heat and cold mirrored the internal currents of struggle and hope that defined his ministry. As the sole compass for the nation's spiritual direction, Samuel bore the fractures and hopes of a people transitioning from tribal judges to a centralized monarchy. This historic moment demanded a voice that could transcend partisan strife and self-interest—a voice that Samuel delivered with unwavering fidelity but at great personal cost. The burden of the divine messenger, therefore, was not merely to speak but to embody the covenant between God and Israel, a living testimony of faithfulness in an age fraught with uncertainty. In the deepest nights, long after the campfire's glow had faded and the stars wheeled overhead in their endless dance, Samuel's prayers took on the cadence of ancient lament and quiet resolve. His words to God acknowledged the loneliness and the pain but also reaffirmed a trust that outlasted human frailty. "O Lord," he might have whispered beneath that vast, inscrutable sky, "though the burden weighs heavy and my voice falters, Your will alone is my guide. Let me be faithful, though the path is lonely, for in Your presence is my strength." The burden of being God's divine messenger was never alleviated by worldly comfort or acclaim. It demanded a surrender so complete that it stripped Samuel of self-interest and personal ambition, leaving in its place a fierce devotion tempered by conscious vulnerability. The prophet's life was a paradoxical dance of visibility and invisibility—always seen as a pillar of strength, yet often invisible in his most intimate struggles. His voice echoed through Israel's hills and valleys, but only the divine truly knew the depth of the solitude behind those prophetic words. Ultimately, Samuel's journey as God's messenger reveals the profound cost and profound grace embedded in the life of a prophet. To carry a message not of one's own making, to speak truths that unsettle kingdoms and hearts alike, is a weight few can bear. Yet in this difficult path, Samuel's story offers a timeless witness to the enduring power of faith and the tragic beauty of a life spent in holy service—empowered beyond measure, yet alone as no other.

Prophetic Confrontations and Counsel

The flickering light of evening candles cast long shadows on the walls of the Israelite court, where the air often brimmed with political tension and spiritual expectation. In these hallowed spaces, Samuel stood as a figure both revered and feared, a man who bore the weight of divine mandates heavier than any earthly crown. The prophet's role was never an easy one — to confront, to counsel, to correct — all in the precarious presence of kings and leaders whose fates hinged not only on their military might or political acumen but on their responsiveness to the voice of God. Samuel's prophetic confrontations with Israel's leaders were defining moments that set the nation's history on a trajectory, moments marked by a divine authority that brooked no compromise. These encounters were never mere conversations; they were the intersections of heaven and earth, where truth pierced through pride and destiny was wrestled from human ambition. The dialogues of these moments were rich in moral gravity, charged with a courage that could neither be softened nor silenced by royal power. To understand Samuel's legacy as Israel's prophet and kingmaker, one must walk through these confrontations — encounter by encounter — and witness the fraught dynamics between divine will and human leadership.***One of the earliest and most dramatic confrontations took place with Saul, Israel's first anointed king. Saul had come to the throne with promise, tall and commanding, endowed with the charisma of a leader ready to unite the tribes. Yet beneath this promising veneer lay insecurities and impatience, traits that Samuel would come to understand with growing sorrow. Their relationship began with honor and hope, but it would soon be tested by decisions that defied prophetic instruction and challenged the very foundation of Israel's covenant with God. It was after a hard-fought battle against the Philistines that Samuel confronted Saul. The king, eager to consolidate his power and demonstrate his zeal, had undertaken a rash act: he offered the burnt offering himself, a sacred duty reserved for Samuel as priest and prophet. This violation of the divine order was Samuel's first test of leadership. "Why have you not obeyed the command of the Lord?" Samuel demanded, his voice steady yet heavy with reproach. His eyes, sharp and penetrating, fixed Saul in place. "You have acted foolishly. You have not kept the Lord's command." Saul's response was a mix of defensiveness and rationalization. "I saw the people scattering, and I said, 'Today the Lord's enemies will be scattered before me, and I will become king over Israel.'" Samuel's gaze hardened. "You have done a foolish thing. You have not kept the command of the Lord your God, which he commanded you. For now, the Lord would have established your kingdom over Israel forever, but now your kingdom will not endure." Humbled and thunderstruck, Saul's heart sank under the weight of the prophetic verdict. Here was the moment that exposed the fragile balance Samuel had to maintain: to be unyielding in the service of God's command while bearing the painful burden of dictating the fate of a king. Samuel was not Saul's enemy, yet he had to speak the uncomfortable and unwelcome truth. This confrontation was seminal. It underscored the prophet's unique position — neither monarch nor mere advisor, but the uncompromising voice of God's law and judgment. Samuel's words echoed beyond that chamber, a divine decree that Saul's disobedience would cost him not only favor but kingship itself.***Another critical encounter unfolded at the height of Saul's kingship, when the prophet was summoned to anoint the future king: David. This moment was laden with tension, for Saul remained on the throne, yet God's spirit was tugging the future into place through Samuel's hand. The private anointing of David, the shepherd boy from Bethlehem, was itself a prophetic act filled with significance. When Samuel visited Jesse's household, the family presented their sons one by one, each seemingly fit to be king in the eyes of man. Samuel's expectations were shaken; Samuel had learned not to judge by outward appearance alone." The Lord does not look at the things people look at," Samuel said wisely. "People look at the outward appearance, but the Lord looks at the heart." When David was finally brought before Samuel, the prophet felt the unmistakable presence of the Spirit of the Lord descend upon the young man. As the oil touched David's head, the solemn gravity of the moment was profound—not merely an act of selection, but a spiritual anointing that would shape Israel's destiny. This instance, though quieter and without the clashes of Saul's court, revealed Samuel's unwavering loyalty to divine guidance over political expediency. His commitment was to God's will first, even when it meant nurturing the rival of the sitting king.***Samuel's interactions with Israel's leaders were not limited to kings alone. He was also frequently called upon to counsel judges, tribal leaders, and the people themselves, especially during times when the fragile fabric of the nation's identity was threatened by disobedience or external danger. During the tumultuous era when the Philistines advanced aggressively, the Israelites cried out in despair, questioning whether their covenant with God still held in their midst. Samuel stepped forward as a unifying voice, calling the nation to repentance and renewal." Gather all Israel to Mizpah, and I will pray to the Lord for you," Samuel commanded firmly. It was an appeal not just for a military alliance, but for spiritual realignment. The people came, and under Samuel's leadership, they fasted, wept, and repented, seeking divine mercy. At Mizpah, Samuel's role transcended that of a mere political leader; he functioned as a spiritual judge, administering justice and facilitating a national covenant renewal. His prophetic authority was felt palpably as he interceded between God and His people, reminding them that their strength lay not in swords or walls but in faithfulness to the Lord. Yet, this role was fraught with difficulty. Samuel had to navigate between the popular pressure to appease their enemies and the uncompromising call to obedience. His public rebukes were often met with resistance, frustration, and even anger. Once during a gathering, when some elders proposed alliances and compromises that Samuel believed would lead Israel astray, he challenged them directly." Do you think the Lord delights in burnt offerings and sacrifices as much as in obedience to His word?" he asked pointedly. "Disobedience is rebellion, and rebellion is as the sin of witchcraft." This boldness was characteristic of Samuel. He wielded the spiritual authority entrusted to him with clarity and courage, knowing full well the risks of alienating those in power or the people at large. Nevertheless, his allegiance was to God's covenant above human institutions.***Perhaps the most poignant of Samuel's confrontations was his final encounter with Saul, after the king had repeatedly fallen short of God's commands. Samuel was sent to tell Saul explicitly that God had rejected him as king. The visit was heavy with foreboding." Has the Lord as great delight in burnt offerings and sacrifices, as in obeying the voice of the Lord? Behold, to obey is better than sacrifice, and to listen than the fat of rams," Samuel declared with unwavering seriousness. Saul's posture was defensive, yet tinged with desperation. "I have obeyed the voice of the Lord," he insisted, "I have gone the way the Lord sent me." Samuel's piercing response was devastating: "You have not obeyed the voice of the Lord. Why then did you not obey the voice of the Lord? Because you have rejected the word of the Lord, he has also rejected you as king." The tragedy of this moment struck deeply within the prophet's heart. Samuel was not only speaking for God but was the bearer of a judgment that would dispatch a monarch and ultimately alter the course of Israel. The prophet's role demanded he be faithful to God's word, yet the cost was the rejection of a man he had once anointed with hope.***Throughout these exchanges, the dialogue between Samuel and Israel's rulers reveals not only the prophet's courage but the intricate balance he had to strike—a balance between mercy and justice, patience and firmness, mentorship and rebuke. Samuel's prophetic authority was never a blunt instrument of power but a finely calibrated voice that sought to realign human authority under divine sovereignty. In moments of counsel, Samuel's language was measured but resolute. He spoke not out of personal vendetta or political ambition, but with an ear attuned to the voice of God. His words often carried the weight of impending judgment, but always with the possibility of repentance and restoration. When David was celebrated after slaying Goliath, Samuel recognized the spirit of God moving mightily in the young man and offered counsel tempered with hope for Israel's future. Conversely, when Saul faltered, the prophet's rebukes came as harsh corrections borne out of a deep desire to see Israel thrive under God's blessing. Samuel's prophetic confrontations were thus complex exchanges — sometimes tender, sometimes stern, but always courageous. He navigated the often treacherous waters of power with a steadfast compass: his unshakable commitment to God's covenant. This steadfastness earned him respect and influence but sometimes also alienation and opposition.***One of the most revealing examples of Samuel's counsel comes from his dealings with the elders of Israel when they demanded a king like the nations around them. The people's request stung the prophet deeply. He perceived it not simply as a political shift but as a spiritual compromise, a rejection of the Lord as their sovereign. Samuel warned them in no uncertain terms: "This will be the manner of the king who shall reign over you... He will take your sons and appoint them for his chariots and to be his horsemen... He will take a tenth of your grain and of your vineyards, and give it to his officers and servants." Despite the prophetic warnings, the elders persisted, and God instructed Samuel to comply with their demands. Yet, Samuel's role did not end at compliance. He continued to remind the people of the consequences of their choice, to hold before them the cost of rejecting divine kingship. This episode reveals the difficult position Samuel occupied — a mediator between God's intentions and the will of the people. His confrontation was not merely with individuals but with a collective desire that would shape Israel's future polity.***Beyond political leaders, Samuel also confronted the spiritual leaders of Israel when they faltered. Under the mentorship of Eli, Samuel understood the dangers of corrupt priesthood and spiritual apathy. When Eli's sons abused their sacred office by desecrating the offerings and taking advantage of their positions, Samuel was compelled to deliver a divine condemnation. The words that fell from Samuel in the night's darkness were heavy with moral gravity: "Why do you do such a thing? The Lord will surely condemn the house of Eli." This confrontation was charged with both reverence and resolve. Samuel respected Eli as his mentor but understood that faithfulness to God transcended personal loyalty. To speak the truth in this instance meant to proclaim judgment upon the very priestly dynasty under which he had been raised. Samuel's prophetic courage here was formative for his entire ministry. It strengthened his resolve that spiritual authority must never become an instrument of corruption or self-interest. His relationship with leaders was always framed by this higher accountability.***The moral gravity in Samuel's dialogue was often heightened by vivid imagery and metaphor, rooted in the covenantal language that shaped Israel's identity. He painted pictures of obedience and rebellion as matters not of mere ritual but of life and death, blessing and curse, survival and ruin. When Israel's leaders faltered, Samuel did not shy away from stern metaphors. He compared disobedience to betrayal and rebellion to witchcraft, to underline the spiritual catastrophe at stake. When he urged renewal, he pointed to repentance as the only path back from destruction. His speeches were often communal calls — calling the people, the leaders, and the priests alike to reorient their hearts and live in alignment with God's will. The prophet's voice rang with the urgency of one delivering divine reckoning but also with the hope that through faithfulness, restoration was always possible.***These prophetic confrontations and counsel shaped not only Israel's political landscape but also its spiritual life. Samuel's unique position allowed him to be both judge and intercessor, kingmaker and reprover, a conduit of God's will during a transformative era. The relationships between Samuel and Israel's leaders were at times fraught with tension and misunderstanding. Kings bristled under rebuke; elders chafed at warnings. Yet, Samuel's commitment never wavered. He persevered through loneliness and opposition because his loyalty was not to any man, but to the living God. Ultimately, Samuel's prophetic confrontations reveal the difficult balance required of a leader who must speak truth to power — a balance between courage and compassion, firmness and foresight. In these moments, he exemplified the true nature of prophetic ministry: unwavering faithfulness to God's word, even when it costs dearly, combined with a deep love for the people whom God entrusted to his care. Samuel's legacy as Israel's prophet, judge, and kingmaker was forged in the crucible of these dramatic encounters. Through his courageous truth-telling and spiritual authority, he charted a course for the nation that sought to honor the divine will above all human ambition. His life's work remains an enduring testament to the power and peril of prophetic leadership in times of great transition.

Faith Tested: Moments of Doubt and Resolve

There are moments in every life when conviction is not a steady flame but a flicker wavering in the winds of despair and doubt. For Samuel, the prophet who stood as the solitary compass in a nation adrift, those moments came not once but repeatedly, etched deep in the crevices of his soul. His faith was tested by storms—both external and internal—that threatened to uproot the very foundations of his calling. Within those trials lay a profound narrative of perseverance, a testament to the fragile but enduring nature of human belief. To know Samuel fully is to glimpse that silent struggle—to stand alongside him in the desert winds of uncertainty, to hear the echo of his prayers amid flickering flames of hope and fear intertwined. Samuel's life was woven into a tapestry of tumultuous epochs. He emerged from the shadows of Eli's waning priesthood, a boy consecrated by desperate prayer and divine promise, only to inherit a land fractured by moral decay and spiritual famine. The voices around him were cacophonous—tribal strife, corrupt judges, a people yearning for a tangible king. Yet his own voice within was fragile, tested by the loneliness of leadership and the weight of divine expectation.

The very same voice that once answered "Speak, for your servant is listening" had to learn anew how to listen through the storms that shaped his journey. The metaphor of the storm is perhaps the most telling symbol for Samuel's spiritual wrestling. Imagine a man standing on a cliff's edge, the sky darkened by thunderheads rolling with fury, winds lashing at his cloak, rain slicing across his face. Such was the inner tempest that raged within the prophet's heart. The storms came from forces both seen and unseen: the failures of men he anointed, the tightening grip of fear within the people, the loneliness of a mission few could comprehend. It is in these moments that Samuel's faith was not an effortless certainty but a hard-won resolve, beaten yet unbroken. One of the earliest storms came in the form of his mentor Eli's tragic fall. Eli, the venerable high priest and judge, a guiding figure in Samuel's youth, was not immune to flaws. His blindness—both physical and spiritual—led him to misjudge his sons, Hophni and Phinehas, who desecrated the priestly office with impunity. The news of Eli's death, alongside the defeat at the hands of the Philistines and the loss of the Ark of the Covenant, struck Samuel hard. The prophetic mantle he assumed was suddenly draped with the heavy shroud of failure and national disgrace. It was a moment when the ground beneath his feet seemed to give way, the skies echoed a desolation that tested whether the boy who had once heard God's gentle call could now endure the roar of calamity. In the solitude of those nights following such loss, Samuel must have wrestled mightily within himself. The metaphor of flickering flames illuminates these hours—small, fragile lights barely holding the darkness at bay. Like a candle caught in the breeze, his faith flickered, threatened by the shadows of doubt. Was this the pathway God had intended? Was this the reward for years of faithfully listening and serving? Or was he, perhaps, too young, too fragile to bear the mantle laid upon his shoulders? The subtle beating of the wind—a whisper and a taunt—challenged the very core of his trust. Yet, it is here that Samuel's humanity emerges most vividly. He was not a prophet forged in unbroken certainty; rather, he was a man forged in the fire of trial, his faith repeatedly tested like gold refined in the crucible. His perseverance was not the absence of fear or doubt but the courageous choice to confront them, to remain standing when the storms raged fiercest. Samuel understood that faith was not a shield that promised immunity from hardship but a compass that pointed steadily onward even when the path was dark and treacherous. The desert wind offers another poignant image to capture Samuel's inner journey—the relentless, whispering breath of the wilderness. The desert in which Samuel ministered was not only a physical place but also a spiritual landscape; barren, vast, and often brutal, it mirrored the solitude of his prophetic mission. Much like the windcarved stone untouched by the crowd, Samuel's voice was honed and shaped by isolation. And just as the wind can erode and transform, so too did the challenges he faced sculpt his resolve. One such test of resolve occurred during the transition from judge to monarch, a pivot that tested Samuel's obedience and faith in divine timing. When the people clamored for a king to lead them "like all the nations," Samuel was deeply pained. The request felt like a rejection—not of him, but of God's unique, sovereign rule over Israel. It was an agonizing crossroads: to acquiesce to the people's demand, knowing it marked a significant departure from the theocratic order he had upheld, or to resist a tide that seemed unstoppable . In this moment, Samuel's faith was akin to a flickering flame caught in gusts of disbelief and disappointment. His heart must have wrestled with questions as old as human history — how to reconcile divine will with human agency, how to read the signs of God's plan when it diverged sharply from personal hopes. Yet even amid sorrow, the desert winds carried a clarity: his role was not to dictate God's timing but to act as the faithful instrument within it. Though his soul quivered under the weight of loss, he resolved to obey, an echo of the first words he spoke as a child: "Speak, for your servant is listening." His faith remained steadfast not in the promises he wished to see, but in the promises God made. And so Samuel anointed Saul as Israel's first king, a man seemingly worthy and strong, yet flawed by human weakness. In Saul's ascendancy and eventual failure, Samuel's faith experienced another profound trial. The king whom Samuel had anointed was promised to be God's anointed leader, but as Saul faltered—marked by pride, disobedience, and rebellion—the prophet was thrust into the tempest once more. His prayers, once filled with expectation for renewal, now carried lament and sorrow. It is here that we witness the profound intersection of faith and grief. Samuel's spirit resembled a flickering flame buffeted not only by winds of trial but also by the painful winds of disillusionment. The desert around him felt emptier, the storms harsher. How could a man persevere when the divine promise seemed so eclipsed? Nevertheless, Samuel remained an unwavering pillar, not because his faith was unshakable, but because his love and allegiance to the divine mission transcended even disappointment. Where many might have turned angry or bitter, Samuel chose surrender—to God's wisdom, even when inscrutable. The final, great test of Samuel's faith unfolded with the anointing of David, the shepherd boy who embodied a new hope. This moment was not the triumphant crowning of a flawless hero but a quiet anointing in the shadows—a fragile beginning amid the wilderness. Here, the flickering flame metaphor shines brightest: a small, steady light nurtured against overwhelming darkness. Samuel's faith compelled him to trust in what was unseen, to hope in a future not yet fully revealed. This hope was not naive optimism but a solemn covenant to persevere, to be patient, to wait for the divine timing. These quiet moments—alone with God amid the desert winds—must have been the crucible in which Samuel's faith was tempered and purified. His journey teaches an invaluable lesson: faith is not merely a confident knowing but a continual choosing. It is the repeated act of lighting one's candle when the winds insist on blowing it out, of setting one's feet upon the rocky path when the horizon only reveals shadows, of listening intently when the divine voice is faint or silent. Samuel's story invites every believer to recognize their humanity within the divine narrative. It reveals that prophets, though chosen vessels of revelation, walk the same perilous roads of doubt and resolve that define the human condition. Their testimonies offer no easy assurances but rather an intimate portrayal of faith as perseverance—a flickering flame not extinguished by the storm but illumined because of it. In this light, Samuel is not merely a historical figure or a distant icon of religious authority. He is a companion to the weary, a beacon for the uncertain, a reminder that in the great storms of life, it is not the absence of doubt that sustains us but the courage to stand firm, the grace to persevere, and the quiet belief that even the smallest flame, held steadfast, can transform the night.

Legacy Carved in Stone and Spirit

Echoes Through Ruins

The wind carved its restless song through the remnants of stone—weathered pillars, fractured altars, and the skeletal outlines of walls that had once enclosed places of gathering, worship, and judgment. These ruins stood silent yet eloquent, monuments of a world long departed yet never erased. In the crumbling layers of sandstone and the faint traces of paint peeling from ancient inscriptions, lie whispers of an era shaped by turbulent faith and unyielding resolve. The breeze, picking up grains of dust and scattering them in delicate swirls, seemed to carry with it the voices of a people who once thronged these spaces—voices that had witnessed the rise and fall of kings and kings' makers, of prophets and warriors alike. To stand amid these remnants is to confront the relentless passage of time, whose steady hand has softened the edges of history but not its imprint. The ruins bear the weight of centuries, yet their stones still breathe the profound significance of a past that reaches into the heart of Israel's identity. Here, where Samuel once walked and judged, where the ark might have rested and prayers ascended, the physical decay speaks in paradox to the spiritual endurance of legacy. What remains is fragile and incomplete, yet through these fragments flows a continuity that transcends earthly dissolution. Amid the scattered stones, faded inscriptions etched upon lintels and monoliths offer tantalizing glimpses into the beliefs and struggles of a people attempting to anchor themselves in covenant and law. These inscriptions, fractured by wind, rain, and the slow creep of moss, present cryptic testaments to moments of divine encounter and human sovereignty. The letters, though partially effaced, still hold a kind of stubborn permanence, like echoes that defy silence. Each letter, each line, gestures beyond itself—to the prophet who spoke God's will, to the judges who administered justice, to the people who dared to hope amidst chaos. These tangible markers stand at the intersection of memory and meaning. They are the skeletal framework of story and tradition, carved not just in stone but in the spirit of generations who passed down the lessons and warnings embedded within them. The stones themselves invite contemplation of the paradox that time, while devouring flesh and facade, cannot consume the essence of purpose fulfilled. Samuel's era, situated in a transitional epoch—a hinge between tribal confederacy and monarchy—left a legacy nearly as intangible as the wind that shaped these ruins yet as enduring as the covenant God sealed with His people. Wandering through these desolate spaces, one cannot help, but marvel at the convergence of physical decay and spiritual tenacity. While the altar stones crumble and the beams have long collapsed, the ethos that Samuel embodied remains palpable. Justice, divine calling, and the painful yet hopeful shaping of a nation emerge from these ruins, not as mere history but as living memory woven into the land itself. This interplay invites a meditation on how history is preserved—not merely in relics or texts but in the quiet resonance that reverberates when one stands where witnesses once stood. The vast openness of the ruins contrasts sharply with the immediacy of Samuel's life and mission. His was a time demanding bold decisions and prophetic courage amidst shifting allegiances and the rise of new political realities. Yet the very stones that once bore witness to such moments now seem to soften, their edges rounded by centuries of wind and wear. This is a lesson about the ultimate fate of human constructs: all empires and power structures crumble, and all monuments wear thin. Still, some things— truth, faithfulness, and covenantal promises—transcend temporal boundaries, embedding themselves not only in stone but also in the collective consciousness of a people. The manner in which these ruins surrender their secrets is itself humbling. Unlike dramatic accounts of battlefield triumphs or kingly decrees preserved in royal archives, here there is silence and fragmentation. The challenge lies in listening—to the silent stones and the spaces between—and piecing together meaning from absences as much as from presence. This invites the reader into a sacred kind of archaeology, where spiritual and historical excavation intertwine.

One recalls the biblical accounts that situate Samuel as a figure bridging eras—not merely a prophet, but a judge and kingmaker. His life was lived in an epoch rife with divine-human tension, political upheaval, and social transformation. Yet, today, these ruins offer little glory or certainty, only the fragile continuity of existence. Through this lens, the material remnants—the cracked pillars, the weathered altar steps, the faded inscriptions—become metaphors for the transience that Samuel grappled with and transcended through his faithful service to God's call. Beyond the physical decay lies a richer story: that of a legacy not measured by permanence in stone, but by endurance in the spirit. Samuel's voice, preserved in scripture, echoes far beyond the ruin-strewn hills. His call to Israel—summoning the people back from the brink of moral collapse and backsliding faith—resonates across millennia. These broken stones embody his era's tension between decline and renewal, between human frailty and divine steadfastness. To walk among these ruins is to touch the edges of time itself. The very air seems charged with the memory of prayers uttered here, of proclamations made, and of the silent tears of a prophet who bore the weight of a nation's destiny. The barren altars and worn steps hold stories of sacrifice, repentance, and hope. They remind the thoughtful pilgrim that, while empires rise and fall, God's purpose moves steadily forward, often in ways unseen by the world's historians but etched deeply within the quiet heartbeat of faith. This tension between decay and endurance invites a deeper reflection on the nature of legacy. Physical monuments, no matter how grand, are ephemeral when isolated from the living tradition they symbolize. Samuel's legacy, carved not only in stone, but in the hearts and lives of those who followed, challenges the observer to consider what truly persists beyond the eroding grasp of time. It is the intangible—faith, obedience, truth—that leaves the most indelible imprint upon history. Even the surrounding landscape participates in this dialogue of continuity. The hills and valleys that cradle these ruins are the same terrain over which Samuel once moved, proclaiming God's word and guiding a people toward a destiny known only to the divine. The cycle of seasons—the relentless sweep of sun and storm—mirrors the rhythmic passage of judgment, fall, and restoration that marked Samuel's leadership and the nation's experience. As the sun dips below the horizon, casting long shadows over cracked stone and weathered inscriptions, a sense of sacred stillness falls. In that lingering twilight, the ruins transform from mere remnants of a distant past into a sanctuary of memory and meaning. Here, history folds into eternity, and the whisper of Samuel's life and mission becomes a clarion call to those who seek to understand the shape of faith in a changing world. Within the stones, within the wind's echo, is a narrative of resilience and hope. Though time erodes all else, the covenant endured; though generations passed, the voice of the prophet remained. To contemplate these ruins is to enter a space both ancient and living—a place where the passage of years illuminates rather than diminishes, where the decay of stone points beyond itself to the unyielding spirit that fashioned them. In this unfolding meditation, the physical markers of Samuel's era serve not as mere relics to be catalogued or admired, but as gateways to understanding an epoch's soul. They invite the reader to look beyond temporal loss, to hear the echoes of a time when one man's faithfulness helped to carve the future of a nation. The ruins and inscriptions, fragile as they are, become vessels of meaning—bridges connecting a past defined by divine-human encounter to a present still shaped by those ancient echoes. Thus, standing amid the ruins, one receives a profound reminder: history is never simply about what remains. It is about what survives in spirit, what endures in memory, and what calls us still to listen and respond. Samuel's legacy is carved not only in stone but in every attentive heart willing to hear the windswept testimony of these ruins and the timeless message they enfold.

Memory and Myth

Throughout the millennia, the figure of Samuel has endured as a monumental presence in the collective memory of faith communities, scholars, and artists alike. His story, rooted in ancient Israel's turbulent transition from tribal confederacy to monarchy, transcends mere historical recounting to become a tapestry where fact and legend interweave, carving a legacy as much spiritual as it is temporal. In this exploration of memory and myth, we undertake a journey through the manifold ways Samuel's life has been preserved, transformed, and mythologized. From oral traditions and scriptural narratives to religious art, each medium shapes and reshapes the prophet's legacy, revealing how history and legend coalesce to inform cultural identity and spiritual understanding. At the outset, it is crucial to recognize that the memory of Samuel did not crystallize as a single, immutable narrative. Instead, it emerged from a dynamic interplay of oral storytelling and written scripture, each influenced by context, audience, and theological intent. The earliest preservation of Samuel's story was undoubtedly oral, transmitted among Israel's tribes before the advent of written codices. Oral traditions bore the marks of communal memory—a fluid mode of preservation that allowed narratives to respond to the social and spiritual needs of successive generations. In such transmission, emphasis was not on exact chronological detail but on the evocative power of Samuel's prophetic role, his unique calling by God, and his anointing of Israel's first kings, Saul and David. These themes resonated deeply with communities wrestling with questions of divine favor, leadership legitimacy, and identity formation amid shifting political realities. Oral retellings would have been shaped by the performative context in which they were shared—sung by bards, recounted by elders, or taught by priests in sacred assembly. The mnemonic devices present in Hebrew poetry, typified by parallelisms and refrains, facilitated both memorization and dramatic effect, ensuring that Samuel's narrative remained vivid and instructive across generations. This living oral tradition provided a foundation upon which later scriptural texts were anchored, preserving not only historical memory but also theological reflection and moral instruction. The transition from oral to written form, culminating in the books of 1 and 2 Samuel, represents a pivotal moment in the mythologization of Samuel's story. Composed and compiled over the course of several centuries, these texts reflect diverse editorial hands and situational concerns. The Deuteronomistic history, which includes Samuel, shapes the narrative with an interpretive lens that seeks to explain Israel's rise and fall in light of covenantal faithfulness and divine justice. Within this framework, Samuel emerges as a liminal figure—prophet, judge, and kingmaker—whose personal integrity and prophetic authority are foregrounded as critical to Israel's destiny. Scriptural authors employ literary techniques that blend historical detail with symbolic imagery and theological motifs. Samuel's miraculous birth to barren Hannah introduces themes of divine intervention and promise. His calling at Shiloh, illustrated with the famous "Here I am" exchanges, dramatizes the intimacy of prophetic vocation. The episodes of anointing Saul and David serve dual functions: narrating the political consolidation of Israel under monarchy while simultaneously underscoring God's sovereignty over leadership selection. Such narratives do not merely record events but interpret them through a theological worldview that encourages readers to see history as the theater of divine action. This sacred text, while considered by many faith traditions as inspired scripture, is not immune to the processes of myth-making. The legend of Samuel grows in the space between literal history and spiritual truth, a phenomenon intrinsic to the transmission of foundational stories. The myth here is not falsehood but rather a narrative form that encapsulates profound truths that transcend the empirical. It casts Samuel as an archetype whose life dramatizes the tension between divine command and human agency, justice and mercy, tradition and innovation. In this sense, the biblical portrayal of Samuel functions as a mythic framework that conveys enduring values and existential questions relevant far beyond its original timeframe. Parallel to the textual tradition, religious art across centuries has further shaped Samuel's mythos, offering visual embodiments of his persona and legacy. From the intricate illuminated manuscripts of the medieval period to monumental sculptures and paintings spanning cultures and epochs, artistic interpretations have enriched popular imagination and devotional practice. These works do not merely illustrate the scriptural narrative but interact with it dialogically, emphasizing particular traits of Samuel—his youth, his prophetic fervor, his judicial authority, or his pivotal role in anointing kings. For instance, Renaissance masters portrayed Samuel with a contemplative aura, often juxtaposed with the young David or the aging Saul, highlighting themes of divine selection and the burdens of leadership. Baroque art might stress dramatic moments such as Samuel's call by God or the anointing ritual, using chiaroscuro and emotional intensity to evoke the sacred encounter. In Jewish art, depictions of Samuel have at times symbolized the covenantal relationship between God and Israel, reinforcing national and religious identity. Eastern Christian iconography likewise venerates Samuel as a prophet, imbuing his image with symbolic attributes like scrolls or lamps that signify revelation and vigilance. The intersection of art and narrative demonstrates how cultural memory reconfigures myth to address contemporary spiritual and social concerns. In times of political upheaval, Samuel's role as kingmaker can inspire reflections on legitimate authority and divine justice; in moments of religious revival, his prophetic voice embodies the call to repentance and renewal. Artistic renditions, therefore, function not only as historical commemoration but as living engagement with Samuel's legacy, resonating with each generation's distinctive context. Beyond textual and artistic media, the collective memory of Samuel extends into liturgy, folklore, and modern reinterpretations, all of which contribute to the complex mythology enveloping his figure. In Jewish and Christian worship, Samuel's story is invoked to exemplify faithfulness to God's call and perseverance amid adversity. The liturgical readings, prayers, and homiletic teachings perpetuate his memory, ensuring an experiential connection between historical narrative and spiritual practice. Folklore and popular imagination, especially in various cultures where biblical stories have been indigenized, often embellish Samuel's narrative with motifs of miraculous signs, divine encounters, or moral parables. These storytelling traditions, while varying in detail, maintain the core image of Samuel as a mediator between the divine and the human, an exemplar of prophetic integrity. In contemporary settings, literature and film have revisited Samuel's story, sometimes emphasizing psychological complexity or exploring lesser-known episodes, thereby renewing interest and inviting fresh interpretation. Embedded within these layered transmissions is the broader phenomenon of cultural memory—how societies remember and reimagine their past to shape identity and values. Samuel's legacy exemplifies the power of narrative memory to provide communities with a sense of rootedness in a sacred history, reinforcing communal bonds and informing ethical frameworks. The mythologization processes serve a dual function: preserving continuity with tradition while allowing flexibility to address new realities. This dynamic interplay ensures that Samuel remains not simply a figure of ancient history but a living symbol relevant to ongoing human concerns. Yet, this blending of history and myth also poses challenges for historians, theologians, and faithful alike. How can one disentangle historical fact from theological embellishment, or reconcile critical scholarship with devotional conviction? The tension between literal historicity and symbolic truth requires a nuanced approach that honors both the evidential basis and the enduring spiritual significance of Samuel's story. Recognizing myth as a vehicle of meaning rather than mere fiction allows for a richer appreciation of the prophet's role in the imagination of generations. Moreover, reflecting on Samuel's memory invites broader contemplation on the nature of prophetic witness and divine revelation. The prophet's life encapsulates the paradox of human limitation and divine empowerment—the fragile vessel chosen for a transcendent mission. In this light, myth and memory become not opposing forces but complementary dimensions through which Samuel's legacy is both preserved and experienced. The mythologized narrative invites believers to participate imaginatively in the encounter with God that Samuel epitomizes, while the historical memory anchors this encounter in a tangible past. In sum, the journey of Samuel's story from oral tradition to scripture, from text to art, and from history to myth, reveals profound insights into the processes by which cultural memory shapes spiritual identity. His narrative exemplifies how foundational figures are continually reinterpreted to meet evolving communal needs, how sacred history is recast in symbolic language, and how myth functions as a conduit of enduring truth. Samuel's legacy, therefore, is carved not only in stone—through ancient manuscripts, monuments, and artworks—but also in the spirit of countless generations who find in his story a source of guidance, inspiration, and identity. As we continue to explore the life and influence of Samuel in the broader context of Israel's history and faith, acknowledging the intricate dance between memory and myth enriches our understanding of his lasting significance. It invites an appreciation for the ways in which sacred stories live, breathe, and transform within the human heart and community, drawing us ever closer to the divine narrative woven through time.

Spiritual Imprint on Israel and Beyond

The spiritual imprint left by Samuel on Israel is undeniable, a legacy that extends far beyond his immediate historical context to influence the very fabric of religious thought and ethical leadership in Jewish tradition and beyond. As a prophet, judge, and kingmaker, Samuel's life embodies a convergence of divine authority and human responsibility, setting a profound standard for the intersection of faith, governance, and morality. His contributions resonate through the centuries, shaping not only the Israelite identity but also offering enduring insights into the spiritual dynamics of leadership and the ethical challenges that confront societies—even today. Samuel's role as the concluding figure of the Judges and the inaugurator of the monarchy exemplifies a pivotal spiritual transition in Israel's history. Before Samuel, the land was marked by fragmentation and spiritual disarray; tribal confederacies lacked a unifying religious or political authority, rendering the people vulnerable and often morally adrift. Samuel's prophetic mission brought both spiritual clarity and political direction. He served as a mouthpiece for Yahweh, challenging the Israelites to remain faithful to the covenant and to recognize the primacy of divine law over human whims or corrupt power. The spiritual imprint of Samuel is foremost evident in his unwavering commitment to the sovereignty of God amid changing political realities. When Israel demanded a king, a desire spurred by social and military pressures, Samuel responded with a nuanced faithfulness that defined the balance between divine prerogative and popular will. He warned the people of the dangers of monarchy—its potential for oppression and deviation from God's commands—while nevertheless anointing Saul as their first king. This act did not represent a capitulation to popular demand but a prudent exercise of prophetic discernment. Samuel's leadership underscored that no human ruler stands above the divine covenant and that submission to God's law must ultimately guide political authority. This principle of accountable leadership remains one of Samuel's most significant spiritual legacies. It forms a foundational ethical framework within the Hebrew Bible and Jewish political theology. Leaders are not sovereign in their own right but are entrusted stewards, accountable to both the divine will and the welfare of their people. Samuel's example—chastising Saul when he transgressed God's commands, rebuking Israel's fickleness, and urging repentance—demonstrates the prophet's role as moral compass and corrective voice. In this way, Samuel's life teaches that true leadership requires moral courage, the willingness to confront injustice, and fidelity to higher principles, even when such stands provoke conflict with popular opinion or political expediency. The prophetic tradition that Samuel embodies also exerts a profound influence on Israelite faith and worship. He stands at the threshold of Israel's classical prophetic era, linking the earlier, sporadic interventions of judges and priests with the sustained, inspired ministry of prophets who follow—figures such as Nathan, Elijah, and Isaiah. The establishment of prophetic authority in Israel restores the people's spiritual vitality by articulating God's will, calling for repentance, and advocating social justice. Samuel's ministry illuminated the ethical dimension of faith: religion is not merely ritual but involves covenantal loyalty manifested in righteous living, compassion for the marginalized, and communal integrity. Furthermore, Samuel's close association with the Ark of the Covenant emphasizes his role as a spiritual mediator between God and Israel. The Ark symbolized God's presence among the people; Samuel's conduct in relation to it, including his efforts to safeguard it and his distinctive prayers, centers the recognition that Israel's fortunes are inseparable from its relationship with the divine. This theological motif—the centrality of God's presence and the requirement for holiness before God—permeates later Israelite worship and underpins ongoing Jewish spirituality. Beyond Israel, Samuel's influence reverberates throughout the wider religious world. His model of prophetic leadership has informed Christian and Islamic understandings of God's messengers. In Christianity, Samuel prefigures the role of John the Baptist and other prophetic figures who challenge secular power and call for repentance and spiritual renewal. His anointing of kings foreshadows messianic expectations centered on anointed leaders bringing salvation and justice. Samuel's emphasis on heartfelt obedience rather than empty sacrifice resonates with New Testament themes that prioritize inner transformation over ritual formalism. Similarly, in Islamic tradition, Samuel is recognized as a righteous prophet who delivered God's message to his people and upheld divine law. His emphasis on moral rectitude and social justice parallels core Qur'anic injunctions concerning the prophetic duty to guide humanity towards monotheism and ethical living. Thus, Samuel serves as a spiritual archetype whose life bridges Abrahamic faiths, illustrating a shared heritage of prophetic authority rooted in divine mandate and ethical responsibility. In the broader discourse on leadership and moral courage across history and culture, Samuel's legacy offers timeless insights. His life confronts the paradox faced by many leaders: the tension between serving the people's immediate demands and adhering to enduring ethical and spiritual principles. His example underscores that leadership divorced from moral integrity risks despotism and social decay. Conversely, leadership grounded in accountability to higher values fosters justice, unity, and flourishing. Samuel's courage in confronting Saul, despite the political costs, embodies the ethical bravery required to sustain righteous leadership. It challenges contemporary leaders to exercise discernment and conscience, standing firm against corruption, populism, or expediency that undermines justice and truth. This legacy invites present-day readers—whether in political, religious, or social spheres—to reflect on the ethical dimensions of power and the necessity of prophetic voices who hold authority accountable. Moreover, Samuel's synthesis of spiritual devotion and practical governance offers a paradigm relevant in today's pluralistic societies. His insistence on the primacy of transcendent values over transient interests speaks to ongoing debates on the role of religion and ethics in public life. By anchoring leadership in covenantal fidelity and moral courage, Samuel sets forth a vision wherein spiritual conviction informs policy, justice, and community life without succumbing to authoritarianism or theocracy. This vision also extends to personal spirituality and communal identity within Israel. Samuel's story exhorts individuals to embrace faith as a living relationship with God that demands ethical behavior and social responsibility. His prayerful engagement with God amid crises models a spirituality marked by dependence on divine guidance and courageous action. Samuel's life thus becomes a call to integrate personal faith with active participation in the pursuit of justice and righteousness. In reflecting on the spiritual imprint Samuel left on Israel, one must also consider how his legacy shaped the prophetic institution itself—often a challenging and lonely role. Prophets like Samuel were intermediaries, bearing the burden of delivering uncomfortable truths, mediating God's justice, and fostering hope amidst judgment. This complex vocation remains a spiritual archetype for those committed to transformative leadership, both within religious traditions and in secular contexts seeking ethical renewal. Samuel's life confirms that true prophecy transcends mere prediction; it involves proactive leadership that transforms a people by reaffirming covenant, challenging complacency, and guiding them toward their divine destiny. This active dimension of prophecy infuses Israel's faith tradition with a dynamic sense of purpose and responsibility that has shaped Jewish theology and the wider Western spiritual heritage. Finally, the spiritual imprint of

Samuel continues to inspire contemporary dialogues on the nature of leadership in a world often marked by moral ambiguity and fractured authority. His example encourages critical evaluation of the sources of legitimate power, reminding communities to root leadership in accountability, ethical courage, and service to the common good. Samuel's legacy invites all to consider that true leadership must harmonize temporal authority with transcendent justice, ultimately seeking the welfare of both people and the divine covenant they uphold. In sum, Samuel's influence is carved deeply into Israel's spiritual and ethical consciousness, establishing him as a foundational figure whose prophetic authority and moral courage shaped the trajectory of Israelite faith and leadership. His life and teachings resonate across religious traditions and historical eras, providing a blueprint for leaders committed to integrity, justice, and spiritual fidelity. His story endures as an enduring beacon, illuminating the path of those who seek to govern with righteousness and serve with unwavering devotion to the moral law engraved not only in stone but in the very spirit of a people.

The Heart's Calling: Lessons from Samuel's Life

Faith and Perseverance in the Divine Journey

In the vast tapestry of faith's journey, there are few lives that so vividly embody the interplay of steadfast devotion and relentless trial as that of the prophet Samuel. His story, as woven through the pages of Scripture and history, is not merely a chronicle of divine commissioning or prophetic authority, but a profound narrative of spiritual endurance. It is a narrative in which faith is both a seed planted in youthful innocence and a flame forged through the tempering fires of doubt, sorrow, and daunting responsibility. To walk alongside Samuel through his challenges and triumphs is to glimpse the delicate yet unyielding roots of perseverance that anchor the soul amid the storms of life, revealing that faith, far from a static virtue, is a dynamic journey marked by continual trust and resilience. Consider first the soil from which Samuel's faith arose. His story begins almost miraculously—the quiet hope of a barren woman, Hannah, whose fervent prayers were answered in the birth of a child destined for divine purposes. This origin alone speaks to the nature of faith as a gift, as well as a responsibility; it reminds us that faith often takes root in the fertile ground of hope against hope, a longing that refuses to yield even when the evidence suggests otherwise. Hannah's prayer, echoing in the silence of the temple, was an embodiment of faith's quiet perseverance. It was a faith that waited agonizingly and prayed silently, yet never ceased to believe in the transformative power of God's promise. From those earliest moments, Samuel's path was shaped by a calling that was as much about listening and discernment as it was about action. As a child serving under Eli, the high priest, Samuel's delicate awakening to God's voice encapsulates a universal truth about faith: it begins with attentiveness. Faith is not a rush toward certainty but a patient listening that invites the divine to speak amid the clamor of doubt and confusion. The metaphor of a still, small voice that calls out in the night—quiet yet unmistakable—captures this essence well. It reminds the faithful that perseverance often means remaining alert and open even when God's direction is not loud or clear. Yet Samuel's journey was not one of uninterrupted clarity. The weight of spiritual and national responsibility soon bore down on him, testing the very core of his faith. He was called to be a judge, a prophet, a leader, and ultimately a kingmaker in a time when Israel itself was wrestling with identity and purpose. His life was punctuated by moments that could have sown despair: the failure of Eli's sons, the spiritual decline of the priesthood, the pressure of an unruly people, and the daunting task of anointing the first kings of Israel. Faith in these moments was not a naive optimism but a courageous resolve—a steadfastness that embraces uncertainty and persists in obedience despite the odds. The story of Samuel highlights a paradox often encountered on the path of faith: perseverance does not guarantee ease or immediate success. Samuel's early experience with Saul illustrates this vividly. Saul was anointed with great promise, a chosen vessel upon whom God's favor rested. Yet the unfolding of Saul's kingship was marked by failure and rejection, causing Samuel profound grief and heartbreak. Here, faith must grapple with the reality of disappointment and betrayal—not only from others but also from the unmet expectations we place on God's plan. Samuel's response was not to abandon his calling, nor to retreat in cynicism, but to continue interceding, seeking God's guidance, and ultimately pressing forward to anoint David, the shepherd boy who would come to define Israel's future. Within this tension between hope and hardship, a profound spiritual lesson emerges: faith perseveres not because it avoids failure, but because it is anchored in the character of God, who is faithful despite human frailty. Samuel's courage in confronting Saul's disobedience and his steadfast trust in God's sovereign purposes teach us that perseverance is nourished by an unwavering focus beyond immediate circumstances—a focus fixed on the divine promise that sustains even when human leadership falters. In reflecting on

Samuel's perseverance, one may liken faith to a mighty river carving its course through rocky terrain. Each trial, each moment of darkness or doubt, is akin to a jagged stone or an impassable cliff. The river's power is not diminished by such obstacles; rather, it is shaped and deepened. It may change direction, it may widen or narrow, but it never stops flowing toward the sea. So too, the faithful journey moves forward, molded not despite the challenges it meets but through them, its depths growing with each encounter of resistance. Samuel's life exemplifies this relentless flow—a faith that bends but does not break, that adapts but does not abandon its destination. It is also important to recognize that Samuel's perseverance was not exercised in isolation. His relationship with God was deeply personal and interactive, marked by prayer, revelation, and moments of heartfelt dialogue. The spiritual discipline of seeking God continually, especially in times of crisis, is a cornerstone of perseverance. Samuel's nighttime encounter with the Lord as a child is mirrored by his mature practice of intercession and discernment throughout his ministry. This ongoing communion forms a spiritual lifeline, sustaining faith through the wilderness and the waiting seasons that characterize any significant divine calling. Moreover, Samuel's journey invites us to consider the nature of spiritual leadership as a crucible of perseverance. Leadership—especially inspired and responsible leadership—is rarely glamorous or free of personal cost. The prophet who speaks hard truths, who bears the burden of guiding a people, who confronts error and injustice, must cultivate a faith that is both buoyant and tough. Samuel's willingness to confront Saul, to rebuke even a king for disobedience, shows us that perseverance includes the courage to uphold truth when it is unpopular or perilous. This kind of faith does not shy away from confrontation but embraces it as part of the divine mandate, living out the conviction that faithfulness to God transcends fear of human opinion. In Samuel's narrative, we also see the profound interplay between human agency and divine sovereignty. His life illustrates how perseverance is exercised within the tension of God's overarching plan and human responsibility. Samuel's obedience to God's word, his proactive steps in anointing kings and judging the land, reveal a partnership of faith where divine guidance calls forth human action. Yet this action is always carried out with reverence for the mystery of God's dominion beyond human control. The faithful do not dictate outcomes but respond faithfully to their calling, persevering in trust that God's purposes will prevail. For modern readers, Samuel's example offers a rich treasury of insights. In moments of personal struggle—be they professional setbacks, spiritual dryness, or relational heartache—his story encourages a posture of enduring faith. The metaphorical language of faith as a seed, a river, a voice in the night, and a courageous leader serves as a map to navigate the inner terrain of doubt and uncertainty. Perseverance becomes a daily discipline of trust, patience, and obedience, a rhythm of persistence that refuses to be defined by failure or fear. Importantly, the spiritual journey is made luminous through community and shared purpose. Samuel's leadership was not solitary; it was embedded within the life of Israel and its unfolding history. His perseverance was nurtured by the prayers of the people and the hope for their restoration. In this, we learn that faith's endurance is often strengthened by connection—by the fellowship of those who share the struggles and victories of the spiritual quest. To persevere alone is to risk isolation; to persevere in community is to find renewed strength. As we ponder Samuel's legacy, the enduring message unfolds: faith and perseverance are inseparable companions on the divine journey. Faith calls us to step forward in trust, even when shadows lengthen, and the path is unclear. Perseverance sustains us through the valleys of uncertainty, inviting us to press on with the assurance that the Great Author of our story is faithful. Like Samuel, we are called to listen closely, to obey courageously, and to hope steadily, knowing that our trials are not the end, but the shaping forces of a life fully surrendered to God. In the landscape of faith, the journey is never easy, but it is always purposeful. The prophet Samuel's life bears witness to this truth with eloquence and power. He stands as a beacon for all who tread the winding road of belief, encouraging every seeker to persevere, to endure, and to keep faith alive through every challenge. For faith that perseveres is not simply belief; it is the triumphant expression of a heart attuned to the divine, a spirit unwavering amidst the tempest, and a soul resolute in the sacred adventure of becoming.

Leadership Rooted in Humility

In an age often marked by the pursuit of power, prestige, and personal gain, the life of Samuel stands out as a profound testament to leadership grounded not in dominance, but in humility. His journey is neither one of flamboyant displays of authority nor relentless self-promotion; rather, it is a story of a man who wielded influence through unwavering integrity, courage, and a steadfast commitment to serving a purpose greater than himself. Through Samuel, we glimpse a model of leadership that transcends time—one that challenges contemporary notions of what it means to lead effectively, urging leaders today to balance authority with moral responsibility and to root their power in humility. Samuel's leadership emerged in a turbulent period in Israel's history—a time characterized by political instability, spiritual decline, and social fragmentation. The judges who had preceded him were flawed and often corrupt, and Israel was struggling to find unity and direction. Against this backdrop, Samuel's calling was both divine and daunting. Yet what distinguishes Samuel's leadership is not just his prophetic role but the posture he took toward it: as a servant first and foremost, with an unshakeable dedication to God and the well-being of his people. From the very beginning of his life, Samuel's story embodies humility. The circumstances of his birth—in answer to his mother Hannah's fervent prayers—reflect a recognition of dependence on divine grace rather than human strength. Hannah's vow to dedicate her son to God's service is a powerful symbol of selflessness and surrender, framing Samuel's life from its earliest days as one not of entitlement but of vocation. This early narrative foreshadows the way Samuel would conduct himself: not grasping for power, but accepting it as a sacred trust to be exercised with reverence and restraint. One of the most striking aspects of Samuel's leadership is how he balanced authority with accountability. Unlike many leaders who view their position as an opportunity to impose will unilaterally, Samuel consistently sought counsel from God, genuinely listening for divine guidance before taking action. This speaks to a deeply rooted humility—a recognition that true wisdom and the right path come not from human insight alone but through submission to a higher moral order. His responsiveness to God's voice models a form of leadership that is participatory and reflective, not autocratic. Moreover, Samuel's interactions with the people of Israel further illustrate his servant leadership. He did not isolate himself in distant power centers nor separate himself from the people he led. Instead, he engaged directly with their concerns, judged their disputes, and interceded on their behalf. This accessibility and personal involvement were not signs of weakness but expressions of courageous commitment. Leading was, to Samuel, an act of service, and serving required humility—the willingness to step into the lives of others, to listen intently, and to stand as a mediator between God and His people. Throughout his tenure, Samuel exhibited a moral courage that was inseparable from his humility. In a cultural and political context where power could easily corrupt or intimidate, Samuel remained steadfast, calling kings, priests, and the populace alike back to righteousness. His rebuke of King Saul, for example, demonstrates leadership that does not flinch from confronting wrongdoing, even when it involves those in the highest offices. Facing Saul's rejection and subsequent downfall, Samuel continued to affirm the primacy of obedience and integrity over privilege, revealing a leader committed not to personal popularity but to justice and faithfulness. This courage to speak truth to power, coupled with a humble demeanor, offers an enduring lesson on balancing strength with moral responsibility. Samuel's leadership was not about commanding obedience through fear or force; it was about inspiring loyalty through trustworthiness and ethical consistency. His life challenges the idea that leadership must be characterized by dominance or manipulation. Instead, it proposes a vision where the power of the leader is an extension of their character—tested, grounded, and oriented toward the collective good. Samuel's role as kingmaker further accentuates his commitment to humility and responsibility. The anointing of Saul and later David as kings of Israel was not an act of personal preference or ambition but a divinely directed responsibility that Samuel embraced with solemnity and care. He did not elevate these leaders to secure his own status; rather, he acted as a conduit for God's will, understanding that true leadership is never about oneself but about serving the greater destiny of the community. This aspect of Samuel's story invites modern readers to reconsider leadership ambitions in a contemporary context crowded with self-interest and individualism. Samuel's example reminds us that leadership is fundamentally relational—a commitment to nurture and empower others rather than to elevate oneself. It is a call to leaders across every sphere —political, corporate, social, or spiritual—to root their authority in service and to wield power to foster justice, compassion, and communal flourishing. Another vital dimension of Samuel's leadership lies in his unwavering integrity. In an era where compromises were often the norm for maintaining power, Samuel's life radiates consistency between words and deeds. He practiced what he preached, holding himself accountable to the very commandments he affirmed for the nation. This congruence between principle and practice deepened the trust that people placed in him and cemented his legacy as a reliable and honorable leader. The emphasis on integrity is especially significant when viewed alongside Samuel's prophetic role. Prophets in the biblical tradition were often voices crying out against injustice and corruption, voices that were frequently marginalized or persecuted. Samuel's courage to stand firm in the face of opposition underscores the profound costs that true leadership can demand. Yet it is precisely this willingness to maintain integrity, even at personal cost, that defines the moral core of his leadership. Samuel's humility also manifests in his willingness to step aside when it was no longer his time to lead. After anointing Saul and later David, Samuel did not cling desperately to power or status. Instead, he accepted the shifting tides of history with grace and continued to support the leaders God had appointed. This capacity to relinquish control and empower successors reflects a selflessness often lacking in contemporary leadership discourse. It teaches that true leaders measure their success not by their tenure but by the enduring strength and well-being of those they serve. In exploring the way Samuel's leadership was rooted in humility, several themes emerge that bear directly on modern understandings of leadership:1. **Servanthood as the Foundation of Authority:** Samuel's example dismantles the barrier between leader and follower, replacing it with the notion that leadership is fundamentally about serving others. This counters prevailing leadership models obsessed with hierarchy and control and invites a fresh paradigm centered on empathy, collaboration, and mutual respect.2. **Listening and Responsiveness:** Leadership is not merely about issuing commands; it is a dynamic process of listening—to people, to circumstances, and to transcendent principles. Samuel's attentiveness to God's guidance and the needs of the people demonstrates the power of humility in opening oneself to greater wisdom and insight.3. **Courageous Integrity:** True leadership requires the strength to uphold ethical standards even when it risks unpopularity or opposition. Samuel's unyielding stand before Saul and others illustrates that moral courage is essential to sustaining just and effective leadership.4. **Empowerment and Succession:** Humility in leadership includes recognizing the importance of preparing others to take up the mantle. Samuel's seamless transition of responsibility to Saul and David exemplifies leadership that is less about personal power and more about nurturing ongoing community flourishing.5. **Accountability to a Higher Purpose:** Samuel's deference to divine authority underlines the need for leaders to anchor their vision and actions in principles that transcend individual ambitions. Such an orientation fosters decisions grounded in ethical responsibility rather than expedience. These themes not only define Samuel's leadership but also contribute to a richer contemporary discourse on leadership that emphasizes balance—balance between confidence and humility, authority and empathy, courage and compassion. In today's world, where leadership crises abound—from corporate scandals and political corruption to failures in social justice and environmental stewardship—Samuel's life offers a beacon of hope and a blueprint for renewal. He reminds us that leadership need not be synonymous with ego or coercion but can instead be a vocation marked by humility, honesty, and heartfelt service. His example challenges leaders to reconsider their motivations and methods, prioritizing character and community over personal gain. Moreover, Samuel's leadership provides a corrective to the often fragmented view of power as a zero-sum game. Instead of seeking to dominate or exclude, Samuel's approach reveals power as a gift and a responsibility—one that must be stewarded with care and be conscious of its impact on others. This reconceptualization is crucial for fostering leadership cultures that are inclusive, ethical, and sustainable. We also find in Samuel's story an invitation for leaders to embrace vulnerability. Humility does not mean weakness; rather, it acknowledges limitations and imperfections, creating space for growth, learning, and genuine connection. Samuel's openness to correction, his willingness to act according to divine direction, and his readiness to serve rather than be served all demonstrate how vulnerability can be a source of strength and resilience in leadership. Furthermore, Samuel's leadership bridges the spiritual and practical realms, showing that effective leadership engages the whole person—mind, heart, and conscience. His legacy encourages leaders to cultivate an inner life of reflection, prayer, or meditation, recognizing that true leadership flows from a grounded identity and clear values. In the final analysis, Samuel's leadership, rooted in humility, offers a transformative narrative that challenges prevailing leadership norms and inspires a return to foundational virtues. His life invites each of us, whether in formal leadership roles or everyday positions of influence, to embody leadership that is servant-hearted, integrity-bound, courageously ethical, and deeply humble. As we reflect on Samuel's example, we are called to ask: How might humble leadership reshape our organizations, communities, and nations? What would our leadership look like if it consistently prioritized service over self, integrity over expedience, and courage over comfort? Samuel's life does not offer easy answers but provides a profound and enduring invitation to embody leadership that honors the human spirit and advances the greater good. In embracing these lessons, leaders today can reclaim a vision of leadership that is not only effective but transformational—leadership that embodies the heart's true calling to serve, to uplift, and to lead with humility. Samuel's untold chronicles thus continue to speak across the centuries, urging us to pursue leadership that intersects power with profound moral responsibility, illuminating a path toward a more just and compassionate world.

Hearing and Heeding the Divine Voice

In the vast tapestry of spiritual experience, few themes resonate as deeply as that of hearing and heeding the divine voice. Across ages and cultures, the human heart has wrestled with the profound challenge of discerning when God—or the sacred—breaks through the noise of daily life to call out with a purpose. Samuel's story, which unfolds within the sacred pages of Scripture, offers an illuminating portrait of this timeless struggle and triumph. It is a narrative both deeply personal and universally instructive, inviting all who read it to contemplate their own spiritual journeys, particularly the moments where the heart is stirred by what feels like something greater than itself. Samuel's journey begins in a place that is at once humble and charged with expectation. His mother, Hannah, had longed and prayed fervently for a child, and when he was born, she dedicated him to the Lord's service. This dedication marked the start of a life attuned to spiritual calling, but it was not without its moments of uncertainty and challenge. As a boy serving in the temple under the priest Eli, Samuel's first divine call was initially a puzzling event, almost missed because he did not recognize the voice that called to him in the night. This tender episode holds profound lessons for the spiritual seeker: the importance of attentiveness, the necessity of guidance, the process of discernment, and the readiness to respond. The initial difficulty Samuel faced—confusing the divine voice with that of his mentor Eli's—is something we can all relate to in our own spiritual lives. How often do we misinterpret, overlook, or dismiss the subtle promptings that come in moments of quietness or crisis? Our world, filled with distraction and competing demands, makes the act of truly listening to the sacred voice a formidable challenge. Samuel's experience gently nudges us to recognize that hearing is not only a matter of the ears but a condition of the heart and mind being open and awake. From the outset, Samuel's story underscores that spiritual hearing is often a process rather than a single, magical moment of clarity. When the voice calls, Samuel does not immediately know who is speaking. It is only after Eli instructs him, "Go, lie down, and if the voice calls you, say, 'Speak, Lord, for your servant is listening,'" that Samuel responds appropriately. This act of preparation highlights an essential principle: to hear God's voice clearly, one must be willing to position oneself in openness and humility. The simple phrase, "Speak, Lord, for your servant is listening," is itself a prayer of surrender, a declaration of readiness to heed whatever is to come, no matter how daunting the path might appear. Such a posture— receptive and obedient—is foundational for anyone seeking to understand their calling. It reminds us that spiritual discernment is not about commanding or controlling divine revelation but about creating a space in our lives where the voice of God can be distinguished amidst confusion. The practice of stillness, quiet reflection, and repeated prayerful asking all become tools for deepening this capacity to hear. Here we note an important practical insight: the cultivation of habits that nurture listening is indispensable. Just as Samuel had to be instructed and guided, so too often we need mentors, spiritual companions, or traditions that help us interpret and validate the perceptions we receive. Another valuable lesson from Samuel's experience is the role of persistence. Samuel hears the voice calling repeatedly, and his willingness to respond each time demonstrates the courage and faithfulness required in the often uncertain realm of spiritual calling. The divine voice is not always a booming directive nor a crystal-clear command. It may come in soft whispers, repeated nudges, or through encounters and events that slowly build meaning. Learning to trust the calling requires courage: the courage to take steps forward even when the full picture is not yet visible, the courage to embrace vulnerability in following an unknown path, and the patience to allow understanding to unfold gradually. In this light, heeding the divine voice is always an act of faith. Samuel's immediate obedience—once he understands who is calling—illustrates the ideal response to divine communication. He rises, goes to Eli, and embraces the mission entrusted to him. This act of obedience sets the tone for his lifelong role as prophet and leader. His story suggests that calling is not simply about hearing; it is ultimately about living into what has been heard. To ignore or resist the voice can lead to missed opportunities and heartache; to embrace it, even amid uncertainty, can transform not only the individual's life but the community at large. For the contemporary reader, Samuel's narrative invites deep personal reflection. Where are the moments in your life when you have felt the stirrings of a higher calling, a subtle but persistent prompting that refuses to be silenced? How have you responded—did you seize the moment with faith and courage, or did fear and doubt hold you back? These questions are far from easy because discerning spiritual calling often requires wrestling with uncertainty, overcoming internal resistance, and resisting the temptation to self-dismiss. One of the challenges modern seekers face is the conflation of spiritual calling with external success or clear recognition. Samuel's story quietly dismantles this mistaken notion: his early life was marked by service rather than glory, by waiting in a temple under a flawed priest rather than being swiftly catapulted into leadership. The divine call sometimes asks for patience, endurance, and the willingness to serve in obscurity before the moment of prominence arrives. Reading Samuel's journey reminds us that spiritual calling is less about immediate status and more about faithful stewardship, developing character, and aligning one's life with God's unfolding purpose. A practical dimension emerges here concerning the interior disposition required to be attuned to God's voice. Humility is paramount. Samuel's readiness to listen and obey comes from a heart that is not preoccupied with asserting its own will or agenda but one that is willing to be shaped, corrected, and directed. This posture—a humility born of trust and respect—opens the heart to genuine encounter with the divine. It also fosters resilience, as seen in Samuel's continued service despite the challenging circumstances around him, including the corruption of Eli's sons and the unrest among the people. The call is not always easy or pleasant, but humility allows the servant to endure. Another facet of heeding the divine voice is recognizing that it often calls one beyond personal comfort zones. Samuel's calling meant becoming a prophet and judge at a crucial juncture in Israel's history, roles that would demand courage, wisdom, and sometimes lonely decision-making. For us today, answering the call may mean stepping out of familiar routines, confronting injustice, accepting responsibility for leadership, or living counterculturally. The divine call has a way of unsettling the comfortable and inviting transformation. Spiritually discerning this call involves not only receptivity but also active engagement with the community and the wisdom of others. Samuel's experience illustrates that the journey of hearing and obeying the divine voice is not purely individualistic. Eli's role as mentor and guide was crucial in helping Samuel interpret and respond correctly. This relationship offers an enduring model: spiritual discernment thrives best when it is supported by trusted guides, whether they be spiritual directors, mentors, or faith communities. We are called not only to listen inwardly but also to test and confirm the calling through dialogue and communal wisdom. Moreover, Samuel's narrative points to the necessity of ongoing prayer and reflection to nurture discernment. His awareness did not remain static after the initial call; it deepened and matured over time, shaped by continuous conversation with God and involvement in the life of the nation. For contemporary readers, this aspect underscores that hearing and heeding the divine voice is a lifelong process rather than a singular event. It invites the faithful to cultivate spiritual disciplines—such as prayer, meditation, fasting, or study—not merely as ritual, but as dynamic encounter points where the heart remains sensitive and responsive. Within these spiritual practices, silence emerges as an essential ingredient. The noise of modern life, with its relentless demands and distractions, makes silence—both external and internal—a precious commodity. Samuel's pivotal moment came in the stillness of night, a time when the external world quieted enough for the inner call to become audible. Finding such spaces in everyday life requires intentionality but yields rich reward. It is within silence, away from the clamoring of worldly concerns, that the spiritual voice can be more clearly heard. Finally, Samuel's story reminds us that hearing and heeding the divine voice involves courage to act faithfully even when the path ahead is uncertain or fraught with difficulties. His life was not insulated from hardship; he faced opposition, rejection, and spiritual warfare, yet he remained steadfast in his calling. This courage is born from trust—that the call heard is not a burden imposed but a sacred invitation to co-create with God the unfolding of redemption and hope. In synthesizing these rich lessons from Samuel, readers are invited into a rhythm of reflection that both honors their own experiences and invites deeper faithfulness. The challenge is often not the absence of a call but the willingness to recognize it, name it, and embrace the path it opens. It is a challenge for which Samuel's example is a beacon: a reminder that God's voice calls persistently and personally, that the heart can learn to discern with clarity, and that the faithful response transforms not only an individual life but the course of history. Hearing and heeding the divine voice, then, is both a sacred mystery and an accessible grace—a divine-human dance that requires openness, humility, courage, and persistent trust. Samuel's journey provides a practical and contemplative roadmap, encouraging the reader to cultivate attentiveness, to seek guidance, to embrace the slow unfolding of understanding, and ultimately to live out the calling with ready obedience. In doing so, one not only participates in the ancient story of divine-human encounter but also becomes part of the ongoing narrative of faith that shapes lives and communities across generations. May this reflection inspire you to listen more deeply, to pray more earnestly, and to step with courage whenever the sacred voice calls your name. For in hearing and heeding, the heart's true calling is revealed—and a life aligned with purpose and grace begins.

Gary E. Risenhoover

Bridging Judges to Monarchs: A Transformative Era

From Tribal Councils to Royal Courts

The sun dipped low over the rugged hills of ancient Israel, casting long shadows upon the narrow pathways of the tribal settlements. Around the flicker of campfires and within the simple enclosures of family compounds, the lives of Israel's people unfolded, rooted deeply in tribal identity and kinship bonds. For generations, their governance had been decentralized, communal, evolving from the desperate need for survival and security among disparate groups scattered across the land. The period of the judges was an era marked by both vibrant independence and chronic instability, where power ebbed and flowed with the tides of conflict and divine intervention. Across the tapestry of Israel's history, this era functioned as an extended, turbulent experiment in tribal self-rule. The "judges," whose title belied the larger scope of their authority, rose intermittently — not as hereditary monarchs but as charismatic leaders, military deliverers, and judicial arbiters. They carried the collective hope of their people, summoned by crises that threatened to sever Israel's fragile unity. Yet, as each judge's tenure faded, the underlying fissures among the tribes only widened; underlying rivalries simmered beneath the surface of their cooperation, and the cry for centralized authority grew louder. This background sets the stage for a transformation unlike any the ancient world had yet witnessed — a decisive shift from the familiar, mosaic-like pattern of tribal councils and communal decision-making to the consolidation of power in a singular, royal court. This evolution was neither smooth nor universally welcomed. It was a rebellion of structure, culture, and faith against the entangling uncertainties of decentralized rule. The defining moments of this transition unfolded amid bustling markets alive with chatter, nervous assemblies fraught with tension, and diplomatic maneuvers that would determine the future of Israel's identity as a nation. In the open-air market squares of Shiloh, where the tabernacle's presence drew pilgrims and traders alike, the air was thick with anticipation and uncertainty. Leather merchants haggled beside grain sellers; children darted between stalls laden with olives, figs, and woven textiles. But beyond the quotidian bustle, a palpable undercurrent of urgency coursed through conversations. The tribes, once loosely united by shared ancestry and covenantal faith, found themselves wrestling with pressing questions — questions of leadership, justice, and survival in a world that was growing ever more complex and dangerous. Tribal councils convened in shadowy groves and stone enclosures, their gatherings reflective of an intimate yet precarious political order. The elders, respected for their wisdom and lineage, debated proposals that were often colored by parochial interests. The nature of consensus in these assemblies was fluid, shaped as much by persuasion and respect as by custom and tradition. Yet, with each gathering, the fissures between tribes became more pronounced. The Benjaminites' pride, the Ephraimites' ambition, the Judahites' emerging confidence—all these dynamics created a political mosaic prone to fracturing at moments of external pressure. The stories of these councils reveal a society grappling not only with external enemies but also with internal discord. The narratives preserved in the biblical account reference segments of fierce debate, vigorous argumentation, and sometimes bitter recriminations. These were arenas where tribal identity and ideology clashed as much as they cooperated, setting the stage for a broader conversation about governance. Could Israel's tribes maintain their autonomy and still defend their collective destiny, or did the moment call for a redefining of leadership that would supersede tribal divisions? These questions were not merely theoretical; they unfolded against a backdrop of constant military threat. Philistines and neighboring peoples, recognizing Israel's fragmented state, pressed in with calculated aggression. The tribes' inability to coordinate effectively in defense underscored the inherent weakness of the decentralized system.

Occasional military victories under the leadership of the judges inspired hope but did not yield lasting peace or unity. Increasingly, the people longed for a leader who could unify the tribes, coordinate defense, and provide a stable judiciary — a king. The demand for a monarchy was as much a political development as it was a cultural shift. It reflected the influences milling beyond Israel's borders, where kingdoms such as Philistia, Moab, Edom, and Aram possessed singular monarchs wielding consolidated power. To Israelite eyes, the political realism of having a king seemed both sensible and inevitable. But culturally and religiously, it presented a profound challenge. A monarchy suggested a departure from the nomadic, clan-based leadership sanctioned directly by divine mandate. It raised questions about the source of authority and the nature of Israel's covenant with God. Within the tribes' council assemblies, voices were split. Some elders recalled the promises made to Abraham, to Moses, to the judges who had wielded God's sword and wisdom. Others focused on the pragmatic necessity of unity to withstand enemies and ensure survival. As the heat of debate rose, it became clear that a new order was dawning — one that would reshape Israel's political, social, and spiritual fabric. Parallel to these political deliberations, the royal courts beyond Israel's borders operated on a different plane altogether. Palaces rose with imposing stone, filled with advisors, scribes, and courtiers. Kings ruled from thrones enshrined with symbols of power, justice, and divine favor. Diplomacy was a delicate and constant game, requiring alliances, treaties, and displays of strength. War was often waged less in open battle than in the shadow-plays of negotiation and intrigue. Israel stood at the threshold of these royal realities. The question was how to navigate this transition without losing the essence of what made Israel unique—a people bound by covenant with Yahweh, distinct from their neighbors both in faith and law. Here, Samuel emerges as a pivotal figure, not merely in his personal story but as a symbol of the struggle between old and new, tribal and royal, covenant and convention. As tribal gatherings morphed into assemblies that would choose a king, the scene was often fraught with tension. The people, represented by elders and tribal leaders, gathered in uneasy unanimity, reflecting a grudging acceptance of a new paradigm. Many feared that a monarchy might supplant the paramount role of the prophetic voice, which had until then guided Israel's society. Others felt worn by years of internecine conflict and external threat, eager for the promise of stability a king represented. Imagine the ambiance as these assemblies met in the great open spaces or under the canopy of fig and oak trees, a custom that echoed Israel's pastoral roots. The crowd was a weaving of farmers, herdsmen, warriors, and artisans — all keenly aware that the decision before them was unprecedented. The elders spoke cautiously, weighing tradition against the pressing demands of political survival. Young men whispered about the promises and perils a king might bring. Women, though less formally represented, influenced discussions through family ties and counsel. Messages were exchanged among the tribes by runners and riders, carrying not only news but also delicate diplomatic overtures. The fragile alliances that had held Israel together were like shifting sands, requiring constant negotiation and reassurance. Summits were convened where feasts and rituals complemented the more formal talks, underscoring the significance of fellowship in fostering unity. The moment of Saul's anointing by Samuel in Ramah stands at the crossroads of this transformation. The hall where the elders gathered was thick with expectancy and a measured anxiety. Delegations representing the tribes' interests debated the merits of this military leader — his courage, charisma, and lineage. Samuel's prophetic authority lent the event a potent religious legitimacy, signaling God's endorsement where human politics previously floundered. Yet, underlying the ceremony was a sense of tension: was the monarchy, with Samuel as its kingmaker, a solution or the opening of a new chapter of uncertainty? Within royal courts, as they began to form in Israel, new social orders arose. A retinue of advisors, scribes, and warriors gathered around the king, replacing the more informal and decentralized structures of the elders' councils. Royal decrees began to override tribal customs, and with the anointing of a monarch came an entirely different mode of diplomacy — one requiring emissaries, treaties, and permanent relationships with neighboring kingdoms. The markets and public spaces reflected this change. Long-established barter and communal sharing began to coexist with the emergence of taxation and tribute systems. Vibrant marketplaces in cities like Gibeah and later Jerusalem grew in prominence, attracting traders from across the Levant. The corridors of power extended their reach into everyday life, influencing the rhythms of trade, agriculture, and social interaction. Parallel to political developments, the arts of negotiation and strategic exchange took on new dimensions. The once sporadic alliances formed for war or need evolved into ongoing diplomatic relationships. Gifts were exchanged not only in ivory or silver but in marriage alliances and military pacts. Israel's kings began to navigate a world of realpolitik, balancing faith, ambition, and survival in ways their tribal predecessors had never had to. This evolutionary leap was watched closely by surrounding nations. The Philistines, once content to raid borderlands, now contended with an Israel that spoke a unified voice, rallied under a king and a court. Diplomacy and war merged in a sophisticated dance, with envoys sent to neighboring courts and spies sent to gauge rival capacities. Yet, internal challenges remained intense. The centralization of power generated resentment and resistance among the tribes accustomed to autonomy. Some viewed the king as a necessary evil; others feared the loss of tribal identity and traditional freedoms. Samuel's own role was fraught with difficulty — as prophet and judge, he had to mediate between God's will and the political realities imposed by his people's desires. The tension between tribal loyalty and national unity also played out in the informal courts that developed within families and clans. Elders still wielded influence, but their authority was increasingly circumscribed by royal law. Disputes that once might be resolved by local council or prophetic decree now came before royal judges. The enforcement of the king's decrees required new forms of administration, heralding the embryonic stage of bureaucracy. Meanwhile, the prophets continued to serve as the moral conscience of the nation, often challenging the king's authority when it diverged from divine commands. This balance of power

— prophet, king, and people — formed a triangular dynamic that would characterize Israel's monarchy and influence its destiny for centuries. Through all this, the people's religious life was interwoven with the political transformation. Pilgrimages to the tabernacle, sacrificial rites, and the reading of the Torah sustained the collective memory and identity. These rituals reminded Israel that political authority was not autonomous but subject to the higher covenantal law given by God. The birth of Israel's monarchy thus reflects the unfolding drama of a people wrestling with survival, identity, and faith. From the intimate tribal councils beneath starry skies to the grandeur and intrigue of royal courts, this period was a crucible of transformation. It set the foundation for Israel's emergence as a unified nation-state, capable of standing among the powers of the ancient Near East — yet always under the watchful eye of their God. The story of Israel's political evolution in this era is not just one of leaders and battles, but of markets bustling with merchants negotiating fortunes, assemblies filled with anxious voices debating a new order, and diplomacy conducted with a wary optimism. It is the story of a people learning to speak with both tribal loyalty and national purpose, negotiating the tension between their past and their future. In this delicate moment, Samuel's leadership carved a path bridging the judges' era with the emerging monarchy. His prophetic insight, judicial wisdom, and political savvy shaped the negotiation between tradition and innovation, tribal sovereignty and royal authority. The echoes of those nervous assemblies and shifting courts reverberate still, reminding readers today that the birth of a nation is never simply a political act but a profound transformation of identity and destiny.

Social and Religious Upheaval

The era bridging the judges and the establishment of the monarchy in Israel was not simply a political turning point. It was, perhaps more profoundly, a period marked by deep social and religious upheaval, a time when the very fabric of Israelite identity was being rewoven in response to internal tensions and external pressures. To comprehend the magnitude of this transformation, one must peer beyond the chronicles of kings and battles into the daily rhythms of life—the marketplaces bustling with trade and gossip, the vibrant festivals echoing with ancient chants and new disputes, and the prophetic voices ringing out in towns and fields alike. These scenes paint a compelling portrait of a society grappling with change, negotiating its traditions, power structures, and spiritual compass amid uncertain horizons. A journey through this transformative era reveals a people caught in the confluence of past and future. The lingering legacy of the judges' decentralized tribal confederation, with its localized governance and diverse cultural practices, was giving way to a centralized monarchy. This transition ignited tensions not only over political authority but over the very nature of Israel's covenantal relationship with God, social hierarchy, and communal belonging.---The marketplaces of Israel during this time were microcosms of the broader upheaval. Picture a crowded square in a town like Shiloh or Ramah, where merchants from distant regions beckoned passersby with the promises of exotic goods—olive oil from the hills of Ephraim, fine textiles dyed with crimson from Edom, and pottery stamped with symbols both old and new. Here, the intersection of commerce and conversation became a fertile ground for cultural exchange and subtle contestation. As farmers brought their grains and shepherds their wool, discussions rose not only around prices but over loyalties and leadership. Some voiced nostalgia for the days when elders and judges settled disputes, wary of the concentration of power in a king's hands. Others argued that only a unified monarchy could protect Israel from the incursions of the Philistines and other neighboring adversaries. In these informal forums, the strains of tribal identity mingled uneasily with emerging notions of national unity. Religious practice, too was unsettled in this era. The tent sanctuary at Shiloh, once the beating heart of Israelite worship under the stewardship of the descendants of Eli, was witnessing a waning influence. The rituals conducted there—offerings of burnt sacrifices, the reading of the Torah scrolls, the celebration of pilgrimage festivals—stood as solemn reminders of a covenant grounded in a lived history of liberation and law. Yet cracks were appearing. Reports filtered through villages of breaches in sacred codes—children neglected the ceremonial washings, levitical duties were half-heartedly performed, and some even doubtless sought out other gods or folk magics in times of desperation. The erosion of proper religious observance did not merely represent lapse in ritual; it was symptomatic of a deeper spiritual malaise that many prophets recognized and decried. The activities of emerging prophetic figures—men and women inspired to speak divine truth amid uncertainty—became crucial in staking out Israel's religious identity. Prophecy, in this period, was more than foretelling; it was a dynamic force of social critique and ethical challenge. Some prophets arose from humble backgrounds, stumbling upon God's call in the threshing floors or quiet hillsides; others served as direct mouthpieces to kings and warriors, their words an unsettling mix of comfort and judgment. The prophets' pronouncements often centered on the community's failure to uphold justice, to care for the widows and orphans, and to remain faithful to the One God who had delivered them. They lamented the creeping corruption among the elites—priests who exploited their positions for gain, aristocrats who hoarded wealth at the expense of the poor. Their voices rang through village squares and near the ruins of altars, shaking people awake to the possibility that political and religious decay were intertwined. Social stratification during this era was becoming more pronounced. The once relatively egalitarian tribal system gave way to emerging class distinctions fueled by wealth accumulation and political alliances. Landowners and warrior elites consolidated power, often through intermarriage and patronage networks, while smallholders and nomadic herders found themselves increasingly marginalized. The marketplace reflected these tensions through disputes and alliances, as those with property bartered not only goods but influence. The role of women in society was similarly complex and evolving. Though the patriarchal norm remained dominant, the stories preserved in oral and written tradition speak of women who exercised spiritual authority and influence—prophetesses like Hannah and Huldah, and figures such as Deborah from an earlier era whose legacy still echoed in these times. At festivals, women's participation in song, dance, and ritual reaffirmed communal bonds, even as daily realities sometimes constrained their freedoms. Within households and public life alike, women navigated these shifting currents, preserving traditions while adapting to new social expectations. Community identity itself was a fraught concept during this transformative period. Tribal loyalties remained strong, yet the looming threat of external domination and the internal push for unity under a monarch recast what it meant to be Israelite. Festivals such as Passover and Sukkot became stages for solidarity, where stories of deliverance from Egypt and wilderness wanderings were retold with heightened urgency and relevance. Through these sacred observances, Israelites reaffirmed their collective memory and the hope that their God would continue to guide them amid change. Yet alongside these moments of unity lay clear divisions. Some clans questioned whether embracing kingship was a betrayal of divine sovereignty. Others embraced it as a pragmatic necessity. These debates unfolded not only in councils and assemblies but also around firesides and olive presses, underscoring how political shifts penetrated daily life. One striking scene stands out from this turbulent epoch: a festival at the high place during the Feast of Tabernacles. The air was thick with the scents of incense, spices, roasted lamb, and fresh figs. Men, women, and children gathered to celebrate, their voices rising in hymn and prayer. Suddenly, a prophet stepped forward—a young man named Samuel, whose voice carried the weight of a new covenant. He decried the corruption among priests and judges, calling the people to repentance and fidelity to God. His words sent ripples through the crowd, challenging elders and commoners alike to reconsider their roles in the unfolding drama of their nation. Through this scene, the complexity of the period is evident: joy and rebellion, hope and admonishment, collective memory and individual accountability converging in a single moment. Samuel's prophetic authority, forged in these social and religious upheavals, would come to define the trajectory of Israel's future. Additionally, the shifting religious landscape necessitated reinterpretations of sacred texts and laws. The early scribes and scholars took on the task of preserving Israel's stories, laws, and prophecies amidst the changing sociopolitical milieu. Their efforts both reflected and influenced popular understandings of covenantal faithfulness and kingship. Texts were copied and adapted, sermons preached and debated, as the community sought to anchor itself in a divine narrative while navigating new realities. Political upheaval also impacted the religious elite. The priesthood, once seen as the undisputed custodians of holiness and ritual purity, faced challenges from emerging prophetic movements that questioned established hierarchies and practices. This tension created a dynamic interplay in the governance of sacred spaces. Some priests resisted the rise of prophetic authority, fearing it would undermine their control. Others aligned with prophetic voices to reform religious life, striving to restore a deeper spirituality amid institutional decay. Furthermore, the uneven distribution of wealth and the growing power of an elite class caused social rifts that sowed seeds of unrest. The common people—farmers, shepherds, artisans—often found themselves squeezed between heavy taxation and exploitation by landlords or military leaders. These economic pressures ignited resentment and sometimes violent protest, adding another layer of strain to already volatile times. Prophets gave voice to these grievances, calling out social injustice as a breach of divine law. In the rural outskirts, traditional tribal customs tangled with new influences. Families endeavored to maintain ancestral ways of worship and kinship, even as market towns and fortresses emerged as centers of royal administration. The tension between periphery and center, tradition and innovation, tribal autonomy and national unity played out in small villages and large assembly places alike. The influence of neighboring cultures weighed heavily on Israelite social and religious life during this period. Trade routes brought foreign ideas, gods, and customs into contact with Israelite traditions, sometimes enriching, often challenging them. The Philistines' imposing presence on the coastal plain, the Canaanite city-states' endurance, and Egypt's intermittent interventions all contributed to a milieu where Israel's identity hovered precariously between isolation and assimilation. Some Israelites adopted elements of other religions—idolatrous imagery, imported rituals—which prophetic voices condemned. These tensions illustrated the difficulty of preserving a pure covenant community in a pluralistic environment. At the same time, the blending of cultures birthed new artistic styles, musical instruments, and culinary delights that reshaped daily living and religious expression alike. Amid these complex currents, Israel's understanding of kingship itself was profoundly evolving. The concept of a divinely appointed monarch, once foreign to a culture led by judges raised by God's Spirit, became an object of fervent debate. Was the king subject to God's law or above it? Would a human ruler enhance or undermine Israel's unique covenant? These questions framed political discourse and theological reflection. The anointing of Saul by Samuel, a watershed moment in Israel's journey, did not merely signify a change in governance; it symbolized the negotiation of divine will, human ambition, and social expectation. Saul's ascent embodied collective hopes for security and justice, yet also raised anxieties about potential tyranny and religious compromise. In conclusion, the social and religious upheaval in Israel during the transition from judges to monarchy was not a simple progression but a multifaceted transformation. It involved shifts in communal identity, power structures, economic arrangements, and spiritual practices. The marketplaces hummed with the voices of change, festivals echoed with tensions and hopes, and prophetic words challenged a people to reimagine their covenantal relationship in a new age. Understanding this epoch through evocative scenes of everyday life allows us to grasp not only the historical realities but the human experiences that shaped Israel's destiny. It was in this crucible of upheaval that the figure of Samuel emerged—a leader whose faith and vision would guide his people through the storm toward a new chapter in their story.

Samuel's Role as Bridge and Beacon

In the tumultuous landscape of ancient Israel, where the threads of tradition and change wove a complex tapestry, Samuel emerged not merely as a prophet but as a living bridge between two vastly different eras. His life and work embodied the transition from the fragile system of the judges, marked by cycles of tribal discord and spiritual wavering, to the dawning age of monarchy, a new political order infused with divine purpose yet fraught with human ambition. To understand Samuel's unique role as both bridge and beacon is to grasp the profound significance of his prophetic ministry — a ministry that transmitted divine authority amid uncertainty and illuminated the path forward with unwavering clarity. Samuel's very presence encapsulated a moment of seismic transformation, not only in Israel's governance but in its spiritual consciousness. The era of the judges was characterized by decentralized leadership, where heroic figures rose sporadically to deliver Israel from immediate crises, only to retreat, leaving the nation vulnerable to recurring cycles of apostasy, oppression, and deliverance. There was no lasting political structure, only a fragile confederation of tribes bound loosely by covenant and tradition. Into this milieu stepped Samuel, the last of the judges and the first of the prophets whose influence extended far beyond deliverance in battle; he was to become a conduit of divine will, reshaping the destiny of Israel with his unyielding voice. From the outset, Samuel's birth itself was a symbol of new beginnings and divine intervention. Born to Hannah, whose fervent prayers pierced the heavens, Samuel's entry into the world was marked by hope in a time of silence and barrenness. His dedication to the Lord at the sanctuary of Shiloh prefigured his lifelong devotion and set a tone of consecration and purpose. This early chapter of Samuel's life signaled a turning point—a dawn after a night of despair—which proved emblematic of the greater transformations he would usher in as a spiritual and political leader. Samuel's role was singular and complex. He was both judge and prophet, blending judicial authority with spiritual insight. Yet this dual role was no mere coincidence; it symbolized a bridge spanning epochs. By fulfilling the functions of judge, Samuel upheld the remnants of the old order, ensuring continuity and stability. Simultaneously, as prophet, he projected a vision of the future, calling Israel towards a new covenantal relationship with God—a future in which monarchy, though foreign to the original tribal identity, would become the chosen means of leadership under divine sanction. In his prophetic vocation, Samuel's voice carried the weight of divine revelation but also bore the human struggles of tempering justice with mercy, authority with humility. He spoke with the resonance of thunder but also the gentleness of a shepherd guiding his flock. His prophetic messages oscillated between stern warnings and promises of restoration, uniting Israel's fragmented psyche with a vision rooted in God's faithfulness. This dynamic duality made Samuel not only a stabilizing force in a volatile political climate but also a harbinger of new beginnings—an agent of transformation who navigated the fragile balance between continuity and change. One of the most vivid images portraying Samuel's role as bridge and beacon is found in the symbolic act of anointing the first kings of Israel. In choosing Saul and later David, Samuel did not merely bestow earthly authority; he transmitted divine mandate, embedding sacred responsibility within the very political fabric of the nation. These acts of anointing with oil functioned as powerful rituals laden with spiritual symbolism—an earthly sign of heavenly endorsement. Through Samuel's hands, the anointed kings became extensions of God's will, charged with the mission to unify and lead Israel according to divine purpose. Yet Samuel's role was not uncritical or unyielding. His prophetic authority demanded accountability from those he anointed and from the people themselves. His rejection of Saul after the latter's repeated disobedience underscored Samuel's unwavering commitment to divine standards over political expediency. Here, the symbolism deepened: the bridge between eras was not a mere passing of a baton but a covenantal testing ground where human leadership was held accountable to a higher law. Samuel, as the sentinel of God's will, refused to compromise, signaling that the new monarchy must align with sacred will or risk collapse. Through his unwavering prophetic voice, Samuel became a stabilizing force during an epoch marred by uncertainty and internal strife. The imagery of him standing alone on the heights of faith, confronting the shifting winds of political and social upheaval, captures his essential role. Like a lighthouse on a stormy coastline, Samuel's voice guided the nation away from the rocks of idolatry, anarchy, and moral decay. His leadership brought coherence to chaos, tying the people to their covenantal identity and reminding them of the divine promises that transcended fleeting circumstances. This beacon-like quality of Samuel's leadership can also be understood through the motif of light piercing darkness—a theme pervasive throughout the biblical narrative and deeply woven into Samuel's story. In an age when faithfulness was dimming and Israel's moral compass faltered, Samuel's prophetic illumination rekindled a communal sense of purpose and destiny. His messages, though often grave, were suffused with hope, revealing that God's hand remained active and that transformation was possible. This illumination was not only spiritual but practical, providing a blueprint for national unity, worship reform, and governance aligned with God's righteousness. Importantly, Samuel's role as bridge and beacon also entailed mediating between continuity and innovation within the religious life of Israel. As the priestly order had long faltered under Eli's stewardship and the corruptions of his sons, Samuel restored the sacred sanctuary, renewed the altar, and reinvigorated the public worship of Yahweh. He navigated the delicate task of honoring the heritage of the past while advocating for reforms that would ensure Israel's faithfulness in a changing world. This delicate balancing act made Samuel a pivotal figure in redefining Israel's identity—not abandoning tradition, but transforming it to meet the challenges of a new era. His mediation extended beyond religious ritual to the social fabric of Israelite life. Samuel's judgments addressed disputes, his leadership unified fractious tribes, and his moral example inspired a collective return to justice and piety. Through these acts, Samuel reasserted the covenantal values that had once united Israel, reminding the nation that beyond kings and battles, their true security lay in obedience to God. This restoration of covenantal consciousness was essential in preparing Israel to embrace monarchy not as a surrender of divine rule, but as an expression of it through human agency. The tension inherent in Samuel's role emerges most starkly in his navigation of Israel's desire for a king. The people clamored for a monarch "like all the other nations," signaling a profound shift from tribal confederacy to centralized power. Samuel's prophetic response was honest and sobering; he warned the people of the potential costs of monarchy—taxation, conscription, and loss of freedoms—but ultimately he conveyed God's concession to their demand. This episode reveals Samuel's role as intermediary between divine ideal and human reality, a figure who both guided and acceded, embodying the delicate balance of leadership in a transitional age. Symbolically, this moment captures the essence of Samuel as a bridge: he stood at the crossroads of divine command and popular will, mediating between God's perfect plan and Israel's imperfect desires. His voice rang out not in mere obedience to– but in faithful stewardship of– divine revelation, echoing the complexities of leadership where divine authority intersects with the realities of governance. Samuel's prophetic leadership, therefore, cannot be simplified as mere compliance or rebellion; it was a nuanced engagement with the unfolding plan of God in history. As much as Samuel fulfilled his role as a bridge, his life and ministry also shone as a beacon pointing toward the future. In the anointing of David, Samuel's hands shaped the destiny of Israel's most iconic king, whose reign would consummate the hopes and promises that had been gestating through the ages. This moment symbolized not only the rise of a new political leader but the inauguration of a messianic trajectory that would echo throughout biblical history. Samuel's prophetic insight perceived in David the potential for a Davidic dynasty under God's favor—a dynasty that would extend beyond the immediate political realities and into the realm of divine covenant. The imagery of Samuel anointing a humble shepherd boy, anointing one seemingly unlikely to rule, speaks powerfully to the theme of divine choice overturning human expectations. It encapsulates the prophetic motif of God's ways being higher than human ways, where true leadership arises not from worldly power or charisma but from God's sovereign selection. Samuel, as the bearer of this secret knowledge, thus becomes a luminous figure leading Israel from the shadows of uncertainty into the dawn of hope. Moreover, Samuel's role as a beacon extended beyond the immediate political transition; it set a spiritual precedent. His life modeled faithfulness, courage, and unwavering commitment to God's will in the midst of political upheaval and personal trials. Samuel's example inspired future generations of prophets, kings, and ordinary believers, reminding them that leadership rooted in divine authority could guide a nation through the most precarious of times. The prophetic mantle he bore was not confined to his own lifetime but became a torch passed down, symbolizing the continuity of God's presence and guidance amidst changing human institutions. Samuel's story, laden with symbolic motifs—anointing oil, the sanctuary, the horn of oil, topheth altars, and the divine voice calling in the night—resonates with deep imagery that underscores his pivotal role. Each symbol intertwines divine-human interaction and illustrates the transmission of sacred authority through a turbulent epoch. The anointing oil, for example, marks the sealing of God's chosen king yet also serves as a reminder that kingship is not a secular privilege but a sacred trust. The sanctuary represents the meeting place of heaven and earth, the place where Samuel heard the divine call and where the nation could reconnect with God's presence. The divine voice, heard first as a mysterious call in the dark, came to embody God's revelation through Samuel, signaling the continuous presence of divine guidance amid human uncertainty. In conclusion, Samuel's role as both bridge and beacon captures the profound complexity of his life and ministry. He transmitted divine authority at a time when Israel stood on the precipice of monumental change, linking the decentralized era of the judges with the emerging monarchy that would define the nation for centuries. His prophetic voice stabilized a fractured society while heralding new beginnings, offering both warning and hope. Through symbolic acts, prophetic proclamation, and steadfast leadership, Samuel became the living conduit through which God's will was communicated during one of Israel's most formative periods. In Samuel, the past did not fade into oblivion, nor did the future arrive unmoored; rather, the ancient covenant was renewed and reimagined through his faithfulness. As a bridge, he connected eras; as a beacon, he illuminated the path forward. His legacy reminds us that moments of great transition demand leaders who can hold the tension between tradition and transformation and who speak with the authority that comes not from human ambition but from divine calling. Samuel's story thus remains a timeless testament to the power of prophetic leadership in guiding a people through the darkest nights into the dawn of new hope.

Concluding: A Thank You to You

We've reached the end of this wild ride, and I couldn't be more thrilled that you stuck with me till the finish line. This book was crafted as a labor of love and a testament to the power of curiosity and resilience. Your willingness to dive deep, explore new ideas, and embrace fresh perspectives means the world to me.

Throughout these pages, we've shared discoveries, sparked questions, and journeyed through experiences designed to ignite your imagination. I hope you found moments that made you pause, smile, or even see things from a new angle. That's the magic I aimed to unleash — the magic of transformation through knowledge.

Remember, the end of this book isn't really an ending at all. It's a jumping-off point, a launchpad for your own adventures and explorations. Take what you've learned here and run with it, question everything, and keep that fire of curiosity burning bright.

From the bottom of my heart, thank you for trusting me as your guide. I hope this book leaves you inspired, energized, and hungry for more. You are the reason this journey was so worth it.

Keep exploring, keep dreaming, and never stop believing in the incredible power within you to change the world. Until next time, may your life be filled with endless wonder and discovery.

With heartfelt gratitude and endless inspiration,

Gary E. Risenhoover